Foolproof curves

Quilts with Bias Strips & Continuous Paper Piecing

Barbara Barber

C&T PUBLISHING

©2004 Barbara Barber

Publisher: *Amy Marson*

Editorial Director: *Gailen Runge*

Editor: *Liz Aneloski*

Technical Editors: *Gailen Runge and Joyce Engels Lytle*

Copyeditor/Proofreader: *Diane Kennedy-Jackson*

Cover Designer: *Kristy A. Konitzer*

Book Designer: *Rose Sheifer*

Design Director: *Rose Sheifer*

Gallery pages designed by: *Kirstie L. McCormick*

Illustrator: *John Heisch*

Production Assistant: *Matt Allen*

Photography: *Sharon Risedorph*, unless otherwise noted

Published by C&T Publishing, Inc.,

P.O. Box 1456, Lafayette, California 94549

Front cover: *Across the Pond* by Janet Benjafield
Back cover: *Solstice* by Barbara Barber

Library of Congress Cataloging-in-Publication Data

Barber, Barbara.
  Foolproof curves : quilts with bias strips & continuous paper piecing / Barbara Barber.
      p. cm.
Includes index.
  ISBN 1-57120-228-5 (paper trade)
1. Patchwork--Patterns. 2. Quilting. 3. Patchwork quilts. I. Title.

TT835.B2657 2003
746.46'041--dc21

2003014119

Printed in China
10 9 8 7 6 5 4 3 2 1

Contents

Dedication

To my father, Alfred Ploug, Jr., an amazing man

Photography: Karen Moore

Daddy started his woodworking at the same time I began quilting. With fabric, you have some leeway, but with wood there is none— just look at his "really sharp piecing" in wood!

Daddy,
Patricia and I have always been so very proud to have you as our father and most especially over the past few years.

Acknowledgments

I thank Lois Andrews, Julia Barker, Phoebe Bartleet, Janet Benjafield, Sarah Hadfield, Shelagh Jarvis, Marcia J. Katz, Sally Laine, Anne E. McLain, Cathy Corbishley Michel, Anne Ray, Julie Standen, and Cathy A. Tongue for allowing me to use their quilts in this book.

I thank Myra-Jane Ibbetson for allowing me to use her quilts on many occasions, as well as in this book; for her continued support; and for bringing her delightful mother to sample my cakes; most of all for her friendship.

I give a very special thank you to Linda Park for making quilts for this book and working with me over an extended period of time, for listening, and for helping me to see the trees through the forest; all of this stems from a much treasured friendship. Also, I thank Linda for allowing me to be friends with her wonderful cats, Gus and Teddy.

I thank Clive and Pat Dunning, Mary Holloway, and Colin and Marilyn Currill for allowing me to use their quilts.

I give a very special thank you to Colin Currill, without whom my first book, *Really Sharp Piecing*, would never have become a reality. His technical help has always been invaluable and it has been a real pleasure for us to work with him. A banter with Colin is always most enjoyable. Thanks for your help, yet again.

I thank Veronica Gilbert for being such an inestimable treasure in my life, as well as for the quilts she made for this book. Sadly, during the completion of this book, Veronica lost her battle with cancer. Veronica and Jack are in my heart.

I thank my daughter Eliza for her understanding nature and always being willing to lend a helping hand.

To say thank you to my husband and soul mate, Peter, would be inadequate. Not only is he willing do all of my drawings for me, but also continually helps and strengthens every part of my life.

I also thank my dear little doggies, Mildred and Gertrude, for their boundless love and affection and allowing me to gain so much through sharing their lives.

Introduction

This book has its beginnings in my new work, as well as my older work. In Part I, you will find an updated version of my first book, *Really Sharp Piecing*, now out of print. This section shows you the methods I have developed using foundation piecing for full-circle designs. You'll learn to sew curves using techniques that really work; I know because they worked for me. So, you can get rid of your fear of curved seams, once and for all.

As the idea of simplifying curves was formulating in my mind I was working on *Ladybirds*. As my work on *Ladybirds* progressed, the design for the border changed and I began to explore new techniques to bring about this new design.

Fine workmanship has always been important to me and I played with new possibilities to create a fanciful effect in *Ladybirds* that would give it a high-quality finish. An easy method for Curved or Straight-Piece Binding is the idea that grew out of the many hours I spent working on *Ladybirds*.

I could hardly wait to begin sketching new quilts to bring this new Curved or Straight-Piece Binding technique to life. I began to weave in some other techniques from my earlier works as well. The designs were fun, quick, and exceedingly easy; with endless possibilities, allowing even beginners to design and make their very own, highly complex-looking quilts with a superb finish. They don't always want to spend endless hours on accuracy, but would still like to end up with a quality quilt—one you'd be proud to use, but also know that if you choose you could give it away because you won't be giving away half your life with it.

In Part II, the result of using these techniques is quilts that give the appearance of complex curved piecing, without piecing a single curve. Almost all of the quilts in this book can be accomplished by beginning quilters but the techniques will certainly benefit all levels, including experienced quilters. It opens the door to many more adventures in design that in the past have caused many quilters to avoid curved piecing.

My Really Sharp Piecing workshops are probably the ones I have enjoyed teaching the most because they give instant gratification to all students of all levels. At these classes I do, however, give a warning: "*Expect to be confused.*" But then I always follow it up with these words of comfort: "*Don't worry, it will all suddenly become clear,*" and it does!

Every one of life's journeys begins with the first step combined with a great deal of observation. Through my teaching, I have been amazed to see that most quilters, regardless of our final destination, go through stages of development. The manifestation of these steps is as different as we are different individuals but the pattern of discovery is similar. Take each step as you come to it, don't try to run before you can walk, expand your technique abilities to match your expanding imagination, never say "I can't . . ." and enjoy the quilters' journey.

I hope, through the quilts I share with you in these pages, that you not only enjoy making them, but that you go on to use the techniques in ways I haven't even started to think of yet!

Wishing you many happy quilts,
Barbara Barber

Ladybirds, 90" x 90", Barbara Barber, Hampshire, England

Hints, Tips &
Useful Information

Before starting to make any of the quilts in this book, I would strongly advise you to read through the design and techniques chapters. This will give you the best understanding of the whole process. As a self-taught quilter, I can say from experience that some of the very best information I have gained has been gleaned from what may at first appear to be the rather tedious introductory sections of a book.

In this chapter, you will find general information that will help you get the best results with the greatest ease. Following is a list of materials and equipment, as well as miscellaneous information in which you will find hints and tips to make this type of quiltmaking easier. This information is crucial to having success with the patterns.

Materials and Equipment

SEWING MACHINE Foundation piecing has to be done by machine but you can use any age or model.

NEEDLES I use only the sharpest and newest needles for machine quilting. I put needles that are too dull for machine quilting in a small bottle and save them to use in foundation-piecing projects because the needle dulls quickly as you're sewing on paper.

STRAIGHT PINS Good-quality pins will help you piece accurately. The pins I like best are the long, thin ones with flat, flower-shaped heads. They are more expensive but they last a long time and make a world of difference. It is so much easier to work

accurately with these finer pins. Thicker pins tend to make the layers shift as you insert them, even if you've lined up the edges very carefully. This is especially true when pinning through paper.

FABRICS, THREAD, and BATTING The single most important thing to consider with these items is quality. To produce a quality quilt you must start with top-quality materials. Your work deserves it. I love 100% cotton for my work and therefore use cotton fabrics, cotton thread, and cotton batting. You don't have to use cotton, of course, but for me, cotton has such a forgiving nature and is naturally engineered to last a lifetime or two. If all of the materials in a quilt are made of the same content, it only stands to reason that they will wear at the same pace.

As for batting, my personal favorite is Soft Touch by Fairfield Processing. It is 100% cotton with a lovely feel and can be quilted beautifully by either hand or machine.

STARCH I starch all the fabrics I use in almost all of my quilts. If I starch one fabric in a quilt, I starch them all. By doing this I know they will all behave in more or less the same way. Try it once and you will be convinced. Starched fabrics are always easier to work with and the time spent starching will be more than made up for by the time you save in the ease of putting your quilt together. Starch also stabilizes the fabrics, making bias edges much less likely to stretch. One of the other benefits of starching is that for the most part, I can eliminate the step of prewashing the fabrics, since the starching process preshrinks the fabrics, regardless of the type of starch you use. I check for colorfastness on each of the fabrics I have doubts about.

When I first started starching I used a spray starch, but since then I have expanded my range of starching products and techniques. Spray starch is still the most instantaneous when you want to use a piece of fabric right away. I usually spray at least three lighter coats rather than one heavy coat of starch, as I've found the iron likes this method best. Be sure to iron the fabric completely dry after each coat.

A good alternative is to use a dip starch you have mixed. My favorite is a liquid starch diluted 1-to-1 with water to give the strength I desire. You will have to experiment with your particular brand of starch to determine the correct ratio. After mixing, there are several ways I use this liquid starch.

One way is to put some of the mixture in a bowl and immerse the smaller pieces of fabric, one at a time. Squeeze the first piece out and lay it flat on your ironing board. Use the next piece to be starched to dry the starch off your hands before dropping it into the bowl to soak up the liquid while you use the iron to dry the first piece. By working this way you can also keep an eye out for any colors that may run.

For larger pieces, I put the liquid mixture into a spray bottle, put the fabric flat in the bathtub, and spray until wet all the way through, then iron it dry. This works very well on pieces up to about a quarter yard. The only real drawback is the trouble I get into when my daughter Eliza comes in and finds that I haven't washed out her bathtub!

It can be difficult, not to mention very tedious, to starch large pieces using the iron to dry the fabric. If I need even larger pieces, I use yet another method. This method requires a little preplanning, but takes all the bother out of it and produces an excellent result. Cut a piece of plastic several inches larger than the fabric you plan to starch (I use a new, black plastic trash bag) and place it on the floor. Lay the fabric on top of the plastic and spray with starch until completely soaked, or immerse the fabric and then straighten, and spread out on the plastic sheet. Let it dry completely. Move it to the ironing board and use steam with your iron to turn this into a beautifully firm fabric that is ready for cutting.

I only starch the fabric I need when I need it. Estimate the amount you will need of a certain fabric and add a little extra. Cut it off from the bulk of your fabric and starch just the amount you need. Be sure to use enough starch to actually stiffen the fabric and to make sure you dry it completely before cutting. To see the value of using starch, it does need to be stiff. My guide is, the more intricate the work, the stiffer I starch.

The starch does cause a build-up to form on the iron but this is easily removed. Let the iron cool down and then remove the starch with a damp cloth. After starching, be sure to clean the iron *before* pressing fabrics while sewing.

All of the quilts in this book have been made with well-starched, 100% cotton fabrics. Be sure to starch the fabrics before cutting. If you starch a cut piece, it will lose all accuracy.

All of my work is quilted by machine and I do think the starch is an asset to quality machine quilting. However, if you are going to quilt by hand, I urge you to rinse the starch out of the finished quilt top before layering it because otherwise, you will find it very hard to get the needle through the starched fabrics, particularly where there are seams involved.

IRON Do not use steam with starched fabrics or freezer paper. (You should use steam during the starching process, but not once the fabrics are starched.) I like to press each seam as I sew, but if the fabrics are well starched it isn't as vital since the starched fabrics finger-press very well. As for the use of steam, like many quilters, I have a strong personal preference—no steam for me.

DESIGN or PATTERN SHEETS Most of the designs in this book are, at least in part, sewn on paper and therefore you will need adequate copies of each design to make a particular quilt. Some of the designs will fit onto a page and are on the pages dealing with that quilt. Often, the patterns are larger than a page and you will find them on the pullout sheet at the back of the book. *Never* cut into or sew on these design sheets. To do so would mean that you have lost your pattern f or good. Each project will tell you which patterns you need and how many photocopies are required to complete the quilt. If you need to enlarge and glue or tape photocopies together to make a block, do this before starting to sew.

FREEZER PAPER One side of freezer paper is plain paper, which you can mark with a pen or pencil. The other side has a shiny plastic coating. A desired shape of freezer paper can be applied to the fabric, shiny side down, and ironed on. The heat from the iron melts the coating and adheres the paper to the fabric. The paper can later be easily and cleanly lifted off. It can be re-used several times before it loses its ability to stick to the fabric. When I need a template for a large, odd-shaped piece in a quilt, I use freezer paper. It is easy to use, inexpensive, and very accurate.

General Information

FABRIC YARDAGE Nothing is more frustrating than running out of a certain fabric and not being able to buy more of it to finish a quilt. Most of the quilts in this book are of a scrappy nature and running out of a particular fabric for this type of quilt can often lead to some very creative and pleasing results. However, this would not be the case if halfway through piecing a quilt like *Solstice*, page 45, you ran out of any of the fabrics.

PROJECT INSTRUCTIONS Be sure to read the project instructions completely before starting the quilt.

SEAM ALLOWANCE An accurate ¼" seam allowance for piecing is much more important than you might think, especially when doing this type of work. However, the seam allowances for the foundation piecing are not as important, just as long as they are adequate. Most of the quilts have foundation-pieced units or blocks combined with traditionally pieced sections. Using the methods in this book, you can be assured of an accurate ¼" seam allowance when joining foundation-pieced

units to other pieces of the quilt because you will be stitching on a drawn line. For the best results, check that you are also stitching a true ¼" seam when sewing seams that are not stitched on paper. Many problems can be prevented by taking the time to get your seam allowance right.

PAPER REMOVAL Each project will instruct when to remove the paper foundation. Do not remove it before reaching that stage. Learn to look at the paper pattern as more than a stitching guide. It is a very good stabilizer, which should not be removed until it is necessary to do so. This will help to ensure that your edges, whether it is the edges of the blocks or edges of the quilt top, do not stretch out of shape. When designing your own work, you should be thinking along the lines of "How long can I leave the paper pattern attached?" rather than considering how quickly you can remove it. When stitching a quilt that has a long line of paper piecing along the outside edge, as is the case with *A Fishy Affair*, page 40, I leave the paper pattern in place even when I am layering and safety-pin basting the layers together. The paper pattern is finally removed after the center is fully pinned.

NUMBER THE PATTERN You may find it helpful, for the first few times you do this type of piecing, to write your chosen fabric colors directly onto the corresponding pieces of the foundation paper. If you do this for several pieces at the beginning of a unit, it will help to keep it clear in your mind which fabric belongs to which section as you start the piecing sequence.

MIRROR IMAGE Foundation piecing produces a mirror image of the drawn pattern. This has been taken into consideration for the patterns in this book, but is worth thinking about when designing your own work.

CUTTING PIECES The methods in this book use pieces that are cut a bit larger than the pattern pieces for which they will be used. In the cutting instructions for each quilt, the measurements of these pieces will be given. These measurements include the seam allowances and a small amount to allow for ease when piecing. Everyone works in a different way and you may find you want more or less of an allowance for ease. Make a trial piece before cutting out all the pieces for a quilt. If the sizes of the pieces suit you, continue with the same size pieces. If not, make adjustments in the cutting measurements for the foundation pieces before cutting out more blocks. Most quilters will find the allowances given with the patterns to be adequate.

FABRIC STRIPS The quilts in this book use pieces cut to a given size for the paper piecing. However, they could just as easily be made using strips cut to a certain width with the strip being trimmed off as you add each new piece. I prefer to work with pieces rather than strips because they are less cumbersome and allow me to chain piece in comfort. Using strips to foundation piece may be more comfortable for some people and this is another good reason for making a trial block. The amount of fabric required can sometimes be less when piecing with strips. If you are short of a certain fabric, consider using strips instead of pieces.

SIZE OF PIECES When designing your own patterns you will need to determine the size of the pieces to cut for foundation piecing. To do this, measure the width and length of the finished piece. Measure through the longest and the widest part of the piece. To each of those measurements, add a good inch for seam allowances and for ease when piecing.

PIECING ORDER When designing your own patterns, you will need to figure out the piecing order as you plan the design. With straight seams, it is possible to sew seams that have paper foundations on both layers. You cannot, however, sew a curved seam successfully if there is a paper foundation on both layers. There is usually a way to get around it, as I did when sewing the two rings together in the Really Sharp Piecing block on page 21. Try to think of a way that won't end up losing the wonderfully sharp points you piece on paper. This is the reason for sewing the outer ring into the background before joining the two rings together.

STITCH LENGTH Paper piecing is sewn with a very short stitch length to make the removal of the paper easier. Remember to revert to a normal stitch length for sewing seams that are not foundation pieced, since it will make removing the stitches easier if you should make a mistake.

CORRECTING MISTAKES! Even the most experienced foundation-piecer makes a mistake from time to time. Seam ripping is never a popular activity and certainly not when it is foundation stitched using a very short stitch length. Often, the paper foundation becomes torn in the process. Tape any tears with clear tape as soon as they appear. A clear tape will allow you to see the stitching lines.

I use a method of undoing paper-pieced stitching that rarely causes any damage and, once you get used to doing it, is extremely quick and easy. Best of all, I no longer dread these inevitable mistakes.

I use a method of undoing paper-pieced stitching that rarely causes any damage and, once you get used to doing it, is extremely quick and easy. Best of all, I no longer dread these inevitable mistakes.

Lay the foundation unit down on a table with the paper side down. Work the edge of the piece you need to remove free by using small scissors with really sharp points to snip at the first stitches. The stitching will start outside of the seam lines and usually outside of the cutting lines and therefore, if you should nick the fabric when loosening the edge it will not matter; it will be cut off when you are trimming the pieced unit. Using your free hand, lift the loosened edge and then, while holding it up, use the scissors in the other hand to take small, snipping "bites." These bites will just nick the stitches that become visible as you lift the top piece. As one hand is holding the piece to be removed taut to reveal the stitches, the other hand takes a tiny snip with the scissors. Then, use the tip of the scissors to hold the unit down on the table as the other hand gives a little tug to reveal more stitches.

Continue this for the length of the offending seam. Remove the loose threads from the foundation unit. As for the piece you removed, simply use the opposite edge of it as the stitching line and reapply it correctly. You must use small, sharp scissors and take care not to snip the fabrics as you work along the seam. When you get used to it, you will find it very quick indeed.

Recently, however, my entire seam-ripping life was turned upside down! A student in Texas introduced me to the joys of seam ripping with a beard or moustache trimmer. I was intrigued and made trials of my own to find this a wonderful method to deal with an unpleasant but necessary chore. I have a rechargeable beard trimmer and it whizzes through any undesired seam with amazing speed and never damages the fabric.

EASY PAPER REMOVAL The quickest and easiest method of removing the paper is to do it in an ordered fashion. I always remove the ¼" seam allowance section before going on to the center sections. Keep a pair of tweezers handy to pick out difficult bits. Take care not to distort your work by tugging at it.

ROTARY-CUT CURVES When cutting out photocopied templates that have curved edges, a rotary cutter with a small blade works great. The smaller blade will go around the curve better, especially on tighter curves.

IS IT BIG ENOUGH? When foundation piecing, if you are unsure whether the piece you intend to add will be large enough, just hold it up to the light. Look at it from the pattern side. You can see the fabric through the paper and will be able to tell if it will be large enough to cover the piece it is intended for, including seam allowances. Once in a while, a seam allowance as small as ⅛" is fine.

A student in Texas introduced me to the joys of seam ripping with a beard or moustache trimmer.

Part I

Continuous
Paper
Piecing

*Sew full-circle
designs using
continuous
paper piecing.*

Design

This chapter is not intended as a comprehensive guide to pattern drafting; there are already many excellent books covering that subject. My intention is to start you off thinking in new directions, finding new and exciting ways to use foundation piecing.

The best way to start exploring this type of design work is to take a pencil in hand and make lots of rough doodles. As you read this chapter, do so with a pencil and paper. Continually let your pencil discover "what if" by adding new lines or sometimes by taking lines away. Don't be concerned about the quality or accuracy of your rough drawings. That is exactly what they are—rough! However, they serve their purpose and allow you to develop ideas very quickly. At least three-quarters of the rough sketches will come to nothing. Either you won't like the design, or find it boring, or discover that the piecing sequence is not suitable for this foundation method. But, every so often, you will hit upon a real gem that you just cannot wait to start piecing. This is the time to make an accurate pattern.

I am very fortunate in that my husband, Peter, is very willing and able to draw my designs for me on the computer. Since the time my first book, *Really Sharp Piecing*, quilting programs for the computer have improved by leaps and bounds. If you do other work by computer, it really is time for you to consider doing your drawings this way. If you are able, or know someone who is able to draw your designs by computer, then that is the obvious answer. However, a good percentage of people are still likely to draft their designs by hand.

Circular Designs

The drawing below shows a grid that would be used for designing. This grid has been printed full-size on the pattern sheet, which is in the back of the book. It is labeled Design Grid and will get you started drafting your own patterns. The radiating lines are spaced 5° apart, making 72 lines in the 360° circle. The circles are ¼" apart. It is so easy to use the grid that it could be compared to drawing dot-to-dot.

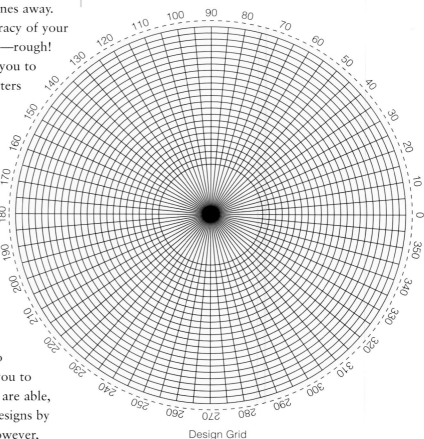

Design Grid

The following five drawings show just how straight-forward it is to draw a pattern for a 2-ring design using the grid. A 2-ring design consists of a center and 2 rings of piecing. In the first of these drawings, you can see the grid with 3 circles drawn on it.

The smallest circle is the appliquéd center. The middle circle shows the edge of the inner ring and the largest circle indicates the edge of the outer ring. For clarity, the rest of the circles printed on the Design Grid have been omitted.

Points are made by drawing angled lines between the circles at regularly-spaced intervals.

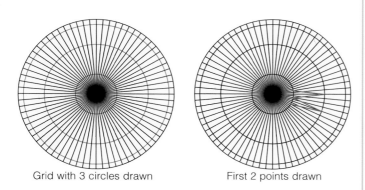

Grid with 3 circles drawn   First 2 points drawn

The number of points you are able to put into a ring depends on the number of radiating lines in the grid. The number of radiating lines in the grid must be evenly divisible by the number of points you want in your ring. There are 72 radiating lines in the grid and 18 points in the ring meaning that, in the example, a point is formed on every fourth radiating line.

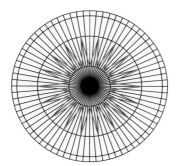

The inner ring is completed by continuing around to form a ring with 18 points.

By following exactly the same procedure, the outer ring is drawn, also with 18 points.

The circles on the grid are ¼" apart and make adding seam allowances easy.

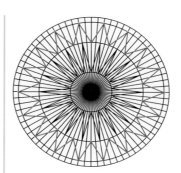 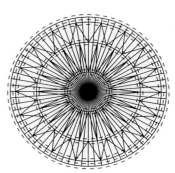

By following exactly the same procedure, the outer ring is drawn, also with 18 points.

Really Sharp Piecing block with its seam allowances added and ready for use.

Square Designs

By placing a square over the grid, you can draw square blocks like the sashing squares for *A Fishy Affair*, page 40.

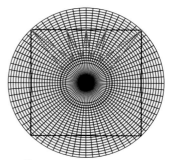

Draw a square on the grid.

The method of drawing is the same as for circles only this time the edge of the outer "ring" will be square. Other shapes can also be used with this grid and hope-fully, as you go through the rest of this chapter, you will start to come up with ideas of your own.

Drawing Designs

To use the grid, either make photocopies of it or use masking tape to hold tracing paper in place and trace it. Do not draw directly on the original grid. The tracing paper has an advantage in that when you are finished with the drawing it will not have all of the radiating lines on it and can be photocopied to produce very clear patterns. If using tracing paper, it is a good idea to trace the circles using a compass to get really smooth lines. When drawing your lines, use a sharp pencil to get fine lines that will produce really sharp points when sewn. I find a mechanical pencil works best for this. A good ruler with tapered edges for drawing will enable you to work accurately.

When using the grid yourself, you will be able to decide the size and number of circles to use, how many points, as well as the shape of the overall design. There are many choices to make, but then that's what designing is all about and the choice is always yours.

The quilts presented in Part I of the book are basically foundation pieced. There is nothing new about foundation piecing and it has been in use since the early days of quiltmaking. Now, it is used more and more to achieve an amazing degree of accuracy. There is nothing wrong with foundation piecing—it is NOT cheating! It is using the techniques and tools available to us in this twenty-first century to our best advantage. When I made *Goato & Friends,* page 61, I did some very complex, traditionally-pieced work to put the overall quilt together. However, I used paper piecing to make the units of bias squares that did, in turn, make the areas that could not be foundation pieced much easier to put together.

Although there is nothing new about foundation piecing, using my methods, even a relative beginner can produce highly complex quilts, very accurately, with ease. What *is* new about my method is that it allows you to foundation piece full circles. You can also piece very long straight units for borders, which are stable and of an exact measurement. The points will be exact every time, whether the strip is made up of spikes or of the triangles in bias squares. Curved units can take on new and interesting shapes.

Foundation-Pieced Designs

In the past, you had to look at a pattern and determine if it could be foundation pieced based on whether or not it had a logical foundation-piecing order and if it had a beginning and an ending. Many designs simply cannot be successfully foundation pieced because of areas where seams intersect or come to a T-junction.

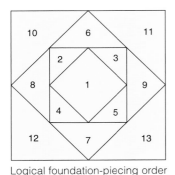

Logical foundation-piecing order

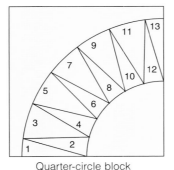

Quarter-circle block

Foundation piecing of quarter-circle blocks, as well as many other blocks, has been in common use for a very long time. They have an obvious starting and stopping place.

Quarter-circle blocks have also been sewn together to form circles. The problem with this method is that's exactly what it ends up looking like—four quarter-circle blocks sewn together. Many times, it can be the only way to achieve a certain effect.

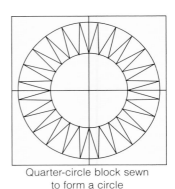

Quarter-circle block sewn
to form a circle

Ring Designs

At other times, the desired effect can only be achieved with a full circle. Using traditional foundation-piecing methods, full circles cannot be foundation pieced because the continuous nature of a circle will not allow for a beginning and an ending, which is necessary for foundation piecing.

However, as shown by the quilts and the techniques in this book, you can cut into a circle, thereby *making* a beginning and an ending, and later rejoin it without compromising the accuracy.

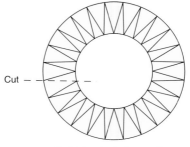

Cut

Cut into circle to create a
beginning and ending.

Any shape that can be foundation pieced in a ring can be considered. *Hexstar* on page 65 is an example of a hexagon shape that has been cut through, pieced in a ring, and rejoined. Similarly, *A Fishy Affair*, page 40, uses a square for the small sashing blocks.

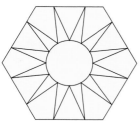

Foundation-pieced hexagon

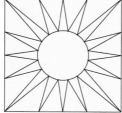

Foundation-pieced square

This same type of spiky star can be inserted into any number of shapes. You can also round off the corners of a square to create a unique look.

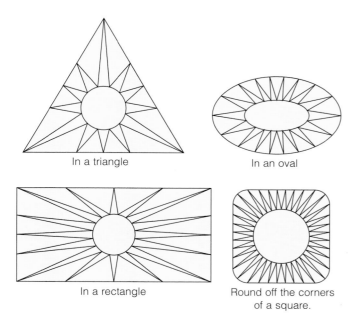

In a triangle

In an oval

In a rectangle

Round off the corners of a square.

Any shape that can be pieced in a ring by cutting into it can be made with this technique.

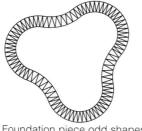

Foundation piece odd shapes

You have so many options when considering this technique. The foundation-pieced ring can be painstakingly drafted with a careful eye on accuracy or a completely free-form design you have drawn using nothing more than pencil, paper, straightedge, and your imagination. The freeform shape on the right is one of a sort that I have been wanting to play with in the Really

Pillow Cover, 15" x 15", Myra-Jane Ibbetson, Dorset, England

Sharp Piecing technique for some time and now I can see using it in combination with the techniques that are introduced in Part II.

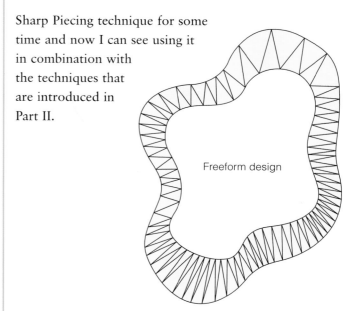

Freeform design

The ring, whatever its shape, will have to have a center that will cover the inside edge of the pieced ring. Remember that the center need not always be a circle and you can use any shape that complements your design.

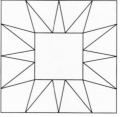

Use any center shape.

Roll'em, Roll'em, Roll'em, 69'' x 94'', Myra-Jane Ibbetson, Dorset, England

Sharp points are very impressive, especially when there are lots and lots of them, but a wedge shape could be foundation pieced into quite an impressive design as well. Try the wedge with a variety of shapes such as circles, triangles, or hexagons.

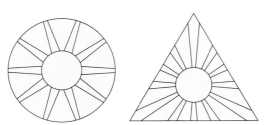

Foundation piece wedge shapes

The inner ring of *Roll'em, Roll'em, Roll'em* was designed with segments that are wedge-shaped and quick to piece, while the outer ring has many small sharp points.

This ring is far more time consuming to sew, simply because of the sheer number of points, but it can be highly effective. It is obvious that this did not put off the quiltmaker, Myra-Jane Ibbetson, because after completing this first quilt, she altered the design and made another quilt called *Rolled'em, Rolled'em, Rolled'em Too Far*, page 62. In this companion quilt, Myra changed the angle of the spokes and spikes, and added a border to produce a variation that I find even more interesting than the first.

Foolproof Curves

The more you work with this type of piecing, the quicker you will be able to get it clear in your mind whether a design can be foundation pieced. Basically, in order for a design to work, you have to be able to add to your "string" of piecing, whether it be a long, straight line of piecing as with *Lilac Feathers*, page 65, or a curved unit, by adding on one piece at a time. Remember to take advantage of foundation piecing whenever possible to assure accuracy in complex designs. When making *Goato & Friends*, page 61, obviously, I was not able to use foundation piecing to totally put the pieced areas together, but where I could, I did. In other words, I used foundation piecing when stitching the bias-square piece-work around each of the animal appliqués.

Detail of *Meridian*, Shelagh Jarvis, London, England

Detail of *Sunflowers*, Cathy Corbishley Michel, London, England

These types of piecing can be foundation pieced very successfully, but only by piecing in a chosen direction. With most ring piecing, it doesn't make any difference which end you start sewing from, but with these it does. Study the piecing sequence in the drawing below to understand how this directional piecing could increase design possibilities in probably every drawing, block, or quilt shown in this book.

Remember to take advantage of foundation piecing whenever possible to assure accuracy in complex designs.

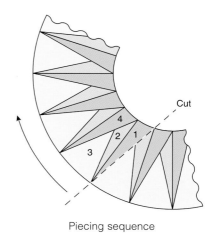

Piecing sequence

By simply drawing a central line through the points you can open many designs to much more color play, whether through contrast or shading, and directional piecing would not be an issue.

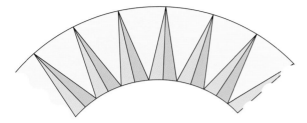

Draw a central line through the points.

A very good motto when doodling for designs is "Let no shape go untried." Very often, the best and the most unusual designs develop from those that you'd originally thought not worth even trying out as a rough drawing. If you don't try it, you'll never know if it had possibilities. This is the same attitude I hold toward the most enjoyable process of auditioning various fabrics to find the perfect one to go in a quilt. I will gladly try out any fabric that has even the most remote chance of working to guarantee that I won't unwittingly bypass the best choice by simply being afraid to try it out. I have certainly made myself look silly many a time by doing just this in quilt shops, but likewise have come up with some wonderful combinations along the way. What is more, I've had a tremendous amount of fun and made many new friends in the process!

By using the techniques for 2-Ring Circular Piecing, page 28, you will begin to think about joining more than two rings together to make a design. Always start with the outer ring and work inward. Working in this way, you can add as many inner rings as you wish and size will probably be the limiting factor in most cases.

Start with the outer ring and work
inward to join multiple rings.

Try varying the width and number of points in the rings. The points in the outer ring could be slender and those in the inner ring wider. This would result in a greater number of points in the outer ring and fewer in the center. The ring with more points will always be a multiple of the number in the ring with fewer. This works for shapes other than circles and unconventional arrangements by working off-center, as well.

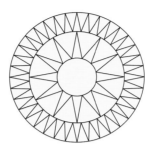

Greater number of points in
outer ring, fewer in center

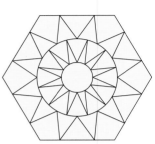

Hexagon

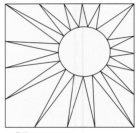

Off-center arrangement

In *Expanding Universe*, page 70, you can see how Myra-Jane Ibbetson has developed the Really Sharp Piecing block using this idea in a highly effective manner.

Although possible, it is not a good idea to design rings of piecing that have points that meet when the rings are sewn together, since it is much more difficult to get those points to come out really sharp because of the bulk where all of the seams come together.

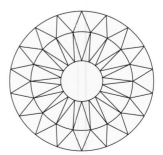

Points should not meet at
ring seamline.

After you have exhausted your imagination for sketching rings, go back and look at them with a new eye focused on color. Try alternating the fabrics around the rings or just throw in the odd one in a completely different color.

Really Sharp Piecing block, 18" x 18", Linda Park, Westborough, Massachusetts

Curved-Unit Piecing

Although foundation piecing quarter-circle units has been around for a very long time, don't limit your thinking to these. In the large block for *Solstice*, page 45, I used two curved units in the same block. One was the straightforward quarter-circle and the other a larger, exaggerated arc.

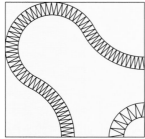

Block with two curved units

When designing curved-unit blocks, remember there are many possibilities for changing the shape of the curved unit. Experiment to find shapes that are pleasing to you.

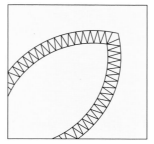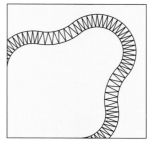

Experiment with curved shapes.

Try arranging the blocks into sets of four to see if any interesting shapes emerge. With both of the above blocks, you would have to consider how to deal with the areas of pieced units that meet when the blocks are sewn together. For the first of these two blocks, it would not be a major problem because there are not that many seams involved. I would certainly consider this design feasible.

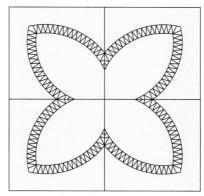

Set of four blocks

When designing block arrangements, watch for areas where too much is going on.

The bulk of the seam allowances can prove to be a real problem if the blocks are left with this piecing arrangement. One possibility is to eliminate some of the spikes at the end of each pieced unit, however, it may not be the look you're after.

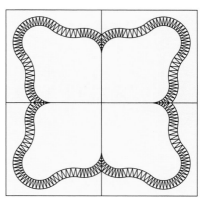

Too much bulk where many seam allowances come together

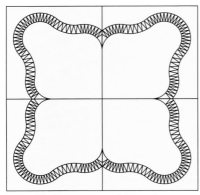

Eliminate some of the spikes
to remove some of the bulk.

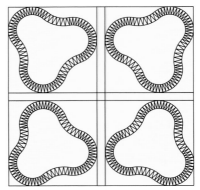

Add sashing to eliminate bulk.

This could also be a problem when grouping blocks with ring units if the pieced edges touch the seams. Even if the area of the seamline where the pieced units touch is short, it could still cause a very bulky seam.

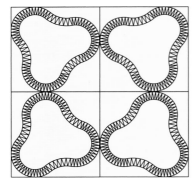

Too much bulk where pieced
units come together

When you come across this type of problem, try looking at an alternative setting. A narrow sashing strip through the middle would solve the problem for both of these designs and could, in fact, strengthen the design through the introduction of another color.

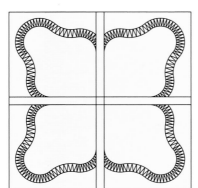

Add sashing to eliminate bulk.

Another solution to consider when this problem involves ring-pieced blocks is to put a margin around the outside of the ring. From my experience, it also happens to be easier to sew a ring into a block that has a margin all the way around the ring, even if it is only a margin of say ¼"–½" wide. There would also be the seam allowance to add on and this would make it possible to work with as little as a ¼" margin.

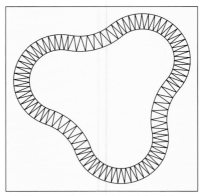

Add a margin around outside of ring.

Design

Design work should be fun and one of the most enjoyable aspects of quiltmaking. If you think, "I'll never come up with my own original designs," you're wrong! That is exactly what I used to think and have come to realize that nothing ventured is nothing gained, and being afraid to even roughly sketch a design will get you nowhere. Yes, there will be times when you come up with ideas that at first will seem impossible to make into a quilt. When designing, whether it be quilts or clothing, a great deal of time is usually spent problem solving. Each time you solve a problem, you strengthen your abilities and become ready to accept even greater challenges.

The Techniques

Stabilizer

You have the choice of using a water-soluble stabilizer such as HTC RinsAway or a paper base for the foundation piecing. Linda used HTC RinsAway for making *Gone Fishin'*, page 80, and saved herself the trouble of having to remove the foundation pattern after completion. She said she loved the stability it gave to the quilt top during the making of the quilt, knowing that it would dissolve when put through the washing machine. When using a soluble stabilizer, there is no need to use anything other than a standard-size stitch, since the stabilizer will be rinsed away rather than being torn away from the stitching.

Photocopies

Photocopies are readily available in a variety of sizes and nowadays the quality of the copies is so true to the original that distortion does not pose the problem it did even just a few years ago. The designs printed within the pages of this book can be made on standard-size copies, but for the larger designs you will need to either use larger copies, glue or tape several copies together, or sometimes both.

When making long, foundation-pieced sections for edges of blocks and borders, gluing copies together is the only sensible solution. I overlap the copies by one square or triangle of the design. This may mean that I use slightly more copies but it will also mean that the finished unit will be more accurate. The beauty of using this method of piecing a long border of bias squares or triangles is that the finished measurement is certain to be exactly what you intended it to be. When gluing together copies that make up a long section, I always number the individual pieces by writing directly on the copies as I glue them together. Always double check the numbering sequence and also be sure to carefully compare the prepared foundation to the section of the quilt you are making. Cutting out the photocopies is detailed with each different technique in this chapter. Do not cut your copies until you have read the instructions for the technique you are using.

If the section or block you want to copy is very large, you may want to consider finding a copier that can make larger copies. This is what I did when making *Solstice*, page 45, since the blocks in this quilt measure $21\frac{5}{8}$" square. On the other hand, you don't have to use very large copies to make *Solstice*. Smaller copies of overlapping sections of the block could be glued together to form the pattern for the whole block. It is important that the copies overlap by at least an inch to ensure an accurate pattern.

Before making many copies for a quilt, make just one copy of a pattern and compare it to the original for distortion. You are likely to get a small amount of distortion on even the best photocopier and therefore it is a good idea to make all your copies on the same machine. Photocopy machines are very good these days and the small amount of distortion has never been a problem for me. Sometimes I have obtained the best results by setting the copier to 99%. This is usually for long, narrow patterns.

After you have found a good copier, get just enough copies to make one block. This block may just be a sample to test out color or may become part of the quilt. By making just enough copies for one block you are able to try it out. You will see if you like the look of it and enjoy sewing it enough to make the whole quilt. Usually you will be so pleased with the fine, sharp points you've achieved that you can't wait to start on the whole quilt. This is the time to return to the same photocopier and get the required number of copies you need to complete the quilt. I always get spare copies to allow for the odd mistake. Most importantly, *always* make your copies from the original pattern. Copies from a copy can lead to a very distorted pattern and very disappointing results.

Instead of getting copies made, you could trace the design. This would be quite time consuming for the whole quilt but not such a problem for a single block. If you do opt for tracing, take care to do it accurately, as a successful outcome depends on an accurate pattern. Again, ALWAYS trace from the original pattern.

Understanding the Full-Size Patterns

In the Introduction, I said, "*expect to be confused.*" I also said, "*it will all suddenly become clear*" and it will! Understanding the full-size foundation pattern can be, and usually is, confusing. Once you are able to view a drawn pattern in the correct way, there is no problem with understanding further patterns. The full-size patterns printed in this book are usually presented as a whole design, rather than with separate templates. The designs could have been printed with all of the sections of the pattern separated, although it would have made a very bulky book. The reason for printing the designs as a whole is because it is actually part of the overall technique and does, in fact, make things easier once you understand how to "read" the design. Also, I feel you will want to be able to use the methods to design and make your own original quilts. When drawing and making your own designs, this system of incorporating the seam allowances into the pattern drawn as a whole will make it quicker, easier, and much more accurate.

When you first look at a full-size pattern that involves circular or curved units, you may think it looks like a maze of lines, while the straight-line units have only one set of lines to define the pattern with no added seam allowances drawn. All *cutting lines* in this book are drawn with *broken or dashed lines*. All *solid lines* on the full-size patterns are *seam lines*. To use the methods successfully, you must get it clear in your mind which seam allowances belong to which unit or piece, and why.

The patterns for these techniques are, in a sense, piled up one on top of another. The seam allowances for one section may, therefore, be printed on part of another section. The paper foundations are cut apart in order to paper piece the individual sections. When piecing a certain section you will often have the dotted seam allowance from another section shown on the section you are piecing. You must come to recognize which seam allowances belong to which sections and learn to ignore them when they appear inside a section you are piecing. If a broken line is *within* a certain section, it will not actually have anything to do with that section. Seam allowances for any piece or section will always be *outside* of the seam line for that area. For any piece or unit, there has to be ¼" seam allowance beyond the drawn seam line. On curved designs, it is easier to draw this on as part of the pattern and then use this broken line to trim the unit after piecing. On straight units it is easier to simply add the ¼" to the solid seam line when trimming the completed unit.

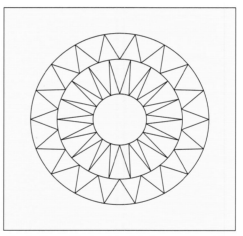

Really Sharp Piecing block in its completed form

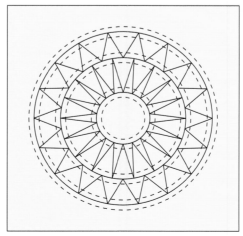

All cutting lines are included
(Figure 1)

Figure 1 shows the way this block would be printed, full-size. Look at the drawing and try to analyze which seam allowances belong to which sections. As you read through the techniques, you will see that a lot of the designs are made using Ring Piecing or Curved Units. The circular block at left is made up of four sections. For this type of piecing you must learn to recognize the different sections of a design and the seam lines that mark where the different sections will be sewn together.

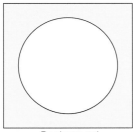

Background

Outer Ring

Inner Ring

Appliquéd Center

Each of these sections has one line in common with the next and that line is the seam line used to join the sections together. Naturally, each of these sections will require a seam allowance in order to sew them together to make the whole. These seam allowances will extend ¼" beyond the seam line.

The outer ring will be pieced onto a paper foundation that has been cut through. It will be foundation pieced as a long, curving strip and then re-joined into a full circle. Seam allowances are required both inside and outside of this ring in order to sew this ring to the other sections of the block. The dotted lines that are ¼" beyond the inside and outside edges of the pieced ring will be the trimming lines after you have completely pieced the ring. This will add the necessary ¼" seam allowances to the ring.

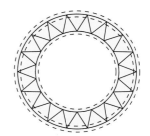

Outer ring with seam allowances

The illustration below shows the outer ring, including its cutting lines, placed on top of the background square with its cutting lines.

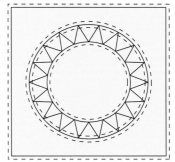

Outer ring with cutting lines on top of background square with cutting lines

It is easy to understand that in order for the finished block to measure 18" square, the background fabric must be cut 18½" x 18½" to allow for the seams around the outside of the block. The circular patterns in this book use squares of a stated size for the backgrounds. You can rotary cut a square of any given size, including the seam allowances, without using a template. Therefore, the square, drawn with its seam allowances, is not a necessary part of the full-size pattern. All of the other lines are necessary.

Get it clear in your mind what each of the lines is used for before going further. At this stage, don't worry about the piecing of the ring, this will be explained in detail later in this chapter. The inner ring will be dealt with in the same way as the outer ring. The inner ring is shown below with the seam allowances added to the outer and inner edges.

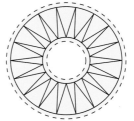

Inner ring with seam allowances added to outer and inner edges

This section of the drawing can now be placed on top of the previous drawing of the outer ring with its seam allowances included.

The appliquéd center will need a seam allowance added around the outside of it.

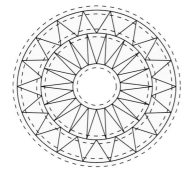

Appliquéd center with seam allowance

Inner ring with seam allowances on top of outer ring with seam allowances

This center section should be added to the rest of the drawing. This pattern is now complete and ready for use.

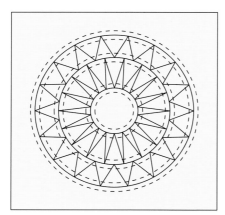

Center section on top of inner and outer rings with seam allowances

There may be times when you want to make a block using only the inner ring of a design.

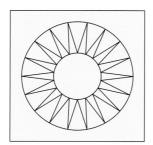

Block with only inner ring

This is the case with *Pumpkin Pie*, page 67. There is no need for a whole new drawing, simply utilize the parts of the drawing you need. The illustration below shows the drawing that would be necessary to make that block.

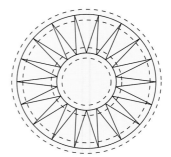

Inner ring and appliquéd center only, including seam allowances

The template for cutting the hole out from the background square would now be made using the second dotted line from the outside edge.

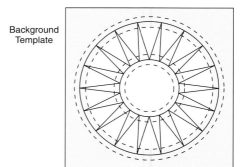

Background Template

Cut background template using second dotted line.

The pattern for a block that is made using Curved-Unit Piecing can be dealt with in the same way. The illustration below shows a curved-unit block without the seam allowances. Look at this block and define the three separate sections of it. The second illustration shows the curved-unit block sections without seam allowances.

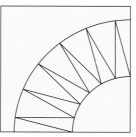

Curved-unit block without seam allowances

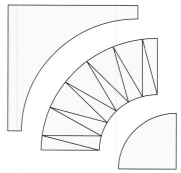

Block sections without seam allowances

Seam allowances are added to the individual block sections. Then, add the cutting lines to the block as a whole unit. The pattern for this block would be presented for use with all necessary seam allowances included.

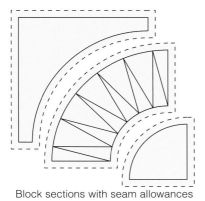

Block sections with seam allowances

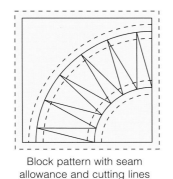

Block pattern with seam allowance and cutting lines

This "piling up" of the pattern is a great help and was not thought up simply as a means of saving space in the book. When I first devised the method for piecing *Solstice*, page 45, this piling up system was part of it from the start. The reason then was accuracy. It's still a good enough reason for me. There is far less chance for inaccuracy if the design is only drawn once. Also, it can be helpful, sometimes, in reducing the number of photocopies you require because sometimes it is possible to use one photocopy for two different parts of the design. In 2-Ring blocks, you can use one photocopy for both the outer ring and the appliquéd center because these sections are not touching each other and therefore, you can cut them apart and use them separately. The same applies to the curved-unit block above. Use two photocopies to make a block. One would be used to foundation piece the curved-unit while only one would be needed to make templates for the other two sections since they do not touch one another. Another very good reason for using this piling up method is that it provides automatic positioning marks which are extremely useful

when piecing the sections together. This will be explained with the piecing.

With an understanding of seam lines and cutting lines, you will be able to apply the same techniques to patterns you have designed and drawn. Take great care when adding the ¼" seam allowances to your own drawings and you should have no trouble sewing them together. After all, your pattern was whole and fitted together properly before you cut it up to piece the units.

The full-size patterns for designs that have Straight-Unit Piecing are easier to understand. They will not include the broken or dashed cutting line and therefore, do not include seam allowances.

Photocopied Templates

I try to use measurements to cut out pieces with the rotary cutter and ruler if at all possible. But this is impossible with oddly shaped or curved pieces. A simple solution I have found is to use photocopies as templates. When I started teaching it, students also found it an invaluable technique. The method may seem a little odd but it does work and is incredibly easy and very quick.

In a nutshell, you staple accurate photocopies onto strips of fabric and cut them out with a rotary cutter. I have never experienced any problems with the stapling and it does not damage cotton fabrics. This method should not be used with thin or delicate fabrics. If you don't want to use a stapler, you can use a large stitch on the sewing machine. This was, in fact, the way I did it when I first started using this method. The stapling came about when I wanted to use larger templates and found that it was difficult to keep the paper templates truly flat on the fabric under the sewing machine.

For most templates the stapling works well, however, if a template is equivalent to an area larger than perhaps a 6" or 7" square, I would suggest that you use the freezer-paper template method given on page 28. This will prevent any buckling that might occur with larger pieces. Remember to include seam allowances when making freezer-paper templates. The quilts that have circular designs will use freezer-paper templates to cut a hole out of the background fabric as detailed in the next section.

2-Ring Circular Piecing

As the name implies, this technique is used for blocks that have two pieced rings.

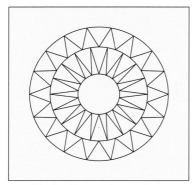

Block with two pieced rings

If, at any time, you feel unsure about what the lines on the full-size pattern mean, refer back to Understanding the Full-Size Patterns, page 24. For my examples, I am going to work with the Really Sharp Piecing design but the methods apply to all 2-Ring designs.

Freezer-Paper Templates and Background

First, make a freezer-paper template to cut a hole out of the background square. This template is only used to make sure that the correct size hole is cut out of the background fabric.

The *cutting line* for this template will be the *second dotted* line in from the outside edge of the design; the dotted line that is ¼" inside the largest solid circular line. This allows for the seam allowance for the curved seam.

1. **Cut out the design slightly larger than the dotted cutting line.**
2. **Glue the wrong side of this copy onto the non-shiny side of the freezer paper.**
3. **Cut exactly on the dotted cutting line.**

If you are doing it correctly, you will be cutting off just the tips of the points in the outer ring.

Notice that, along the outer seam and cutting lines, there are four small lines that indicate the quarter-points of the circle. Two of the four marks will fall on a sewn point and two will not.

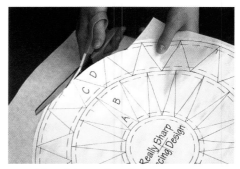

After gluing pattern to freezer paper,
cut on dotted line. Four small lines indicate
the quarter points of the circle.

4. **Cut out the background square the size of the finished block plus ¼" for seam allowances.**

The quilt patterns in this book tell you to cut out squares of certain measurements; these measurements will always include the seam allowances. I spray starch the background fabrics as well as those used inside the block.

5. **Fold the square in half and finger-press the crease along the fold. Unfold and then fold in half in the other direction, creasing on the fold.**

If the fabric has been well starched this should leave clearly visible fold lines. If you can't see the lines with finger-pressing then use the iron to lightly crease the background fabric. This will serve as a positioning guide when centering the freezer-paper template onto the background fabric.

6. **Unfold the fabric, position it right-side up, and center the freezer paper on it, lining up the quarter marks of the template with the folds in the fabric.**

With the background fabric right-side up,
line up the quarter marks of the template
with the folds in the fabric.

Be sure to check for correct orientation as you position the template for each of the blocks in a quilt. In some blocks, a point falls at each quarter mark and thus, needs no special positioning. The Really Sharp Piecing block has points on only two of the quarter marks.

7. Press.

Use the same techniques for making the freezer-paper templates when making half and quarter blocks for quilts like *Roll'em, Roll'em, Roll'em* on page 18. Be sure to add the seam allowance to the straight edge where you cut the circle into a half or a quarter.

In order to position the pieced ring within the block, you will need to mark the background square.

8. Mark each of the points of the design onto the background square around the edge of the template.

These are indicated by the tips that you cut off to make this template. I use a pencil and make one small mark about ⅛" long to indicate each point. I use colored pencils on dark fabrics in order to be able to see the marks.

9. Carefully cut around the template, cutting as close to the template as possible without cutting it.

I make a slit in the fabric using my rotary cutter, large enough to get the scissors through, then cut around with the scissors.

10. Put the square to one side while you piece the rings for the block.

Take care not to stretch the bias edges of the circle. The template can be used over and over until it will no longer adhere to the fabric.

Piecing the Outer Ring

1. Use one of the photocopies to cut out the outer ring for piecing.

Remember to add ¼" seam allowances on both the inside and the outside edges of the ring. If necessary, review Understanding the Full-Size Patterns, page 24. Do not cut exactly on the cutting line but cut roughly ⅛" beyond the cutting line; after piecing is complete you will trim the ring exactly on the cutting line. Don't be tempted to leave a larger margin as this will not help but will, in fact, hinder your piecing. Save the center section of this copy to use when appliquéing the center circle.

2. Cut the ring open by carefully cutting on one of the solid seam lines of the points in the ring.

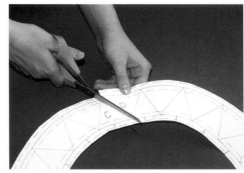
Cut the ring open.

It does not matter which of the angled lines you cut or which end of the ring you start the piecing from unless it happens to be a one-way design such as the Sunflower block, page 19, or *Meridian*, page 62.

This ring is long and difficult to handle. In its present state it will slow you down and could easily get torn apart during the piecing. To avoid these problems, I piece long units, straight and curved, using a "scroll" method.

3. Roll the pattern up with the printed design on the inside. Leave about 5" free at the end and secure with an over-sized paper clip.

Roll the pattern, printed design inside,
and secure with paper clip.

I stitch several pieces, unroll a bit more, and continue. I never have more than about 5" of the unit unrolled at any time because as soon as the pieced end is long enough, I start rolling it up in the same way, forming a scroll.

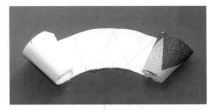
Unroll the pattern and roll the
pieced section as you go.

This way it stays neat and tidy and I find it a pleasant way to work, producing good results. Also, it allows me to chain piece up to 15 to 16 units at a time without them getting all tangled up.

Establish clearly in your mind which cut piece belongs to each section printed on the paper ring. In my example, the first piece could have been either the C or D piece. It happens to be the C piece. This will depend on where the ring was cut and from which end you start the piecing. You may find it helpful to write the piece letter and the fabric color on the foundation paper for the first few pieces of the ring.

Other than when working with one-way designs, it really does not matter which piece you start with except when using a stripe. Striped fabrics can give a really super effect in piecing these designs and there is a very simple method to use to be sure that all the stripes run in the same direction. Do not start piecing the end of the ring where the end piece would be sewn with a stripe piece. The first piece of the ring is dealt with in a slightly different way than all of the other pieces. If you introduce the stripe fabric for the second piece of the ring, you will guarantee that the stripe will remain consistent all the way around the ring.

4. Put the pieces you cut for the outer ring in a handy position for piecing at the machine.
5. Set your stitch size to 1.5 or about 20 stitches per inch.
6. Pick up one of each of the cut fabrics.

The pieces will probably be different sizes regardless of what design you are making. Their lengths may be the same but their widths will probably be different.

7. Place them, right sides together, with the long edges even on one side. Lay them on your sewing machine extension table with the wrong side of the fabric, the first in the ring, on top. Position the rolled paper ring on these fabrics. The top fabric should be just a bit larger than the first piece of the pattern. The first solid line you see will be the first seam line. The seam allowance will be on the rolled side of the solid line. Position the foundation so a scant ¼" of fabric lies beyond the solid

line on the rolled side of the foundation. The ends of the fabric pieces should protrude just beyond the cut edges of the paper ring allowing you to position the fabric without having to hold it up to the light.

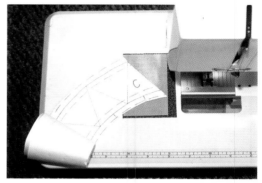

Position the foundation so a scant ¼" of fabric lies beyond the solid line.

8. Hold the foundation firmly in place and slide it over, placing it with the seam line straight in front of the needle.

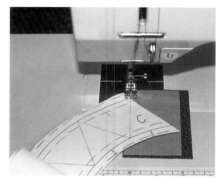

Place the foundation and fabrics in front of the needle.

Remember that it will make it easier to remove the paper upon completion if you lower the stitch size to produce smaller stitches.

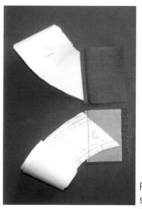

9. Sew from the very edge of the fabric to the other edge and remove it from the machine.

Front and back after stitching first seam

10. Finger-press the pieces open.

Front and back after finger-pressing

11. Trim the fabric very close to the curved edges of the ring. On the short, straight end where you cut through the ring, trim the fabric to about ⅜". After you have finished piecing the ring, this margin will form the seam allowance when the ring is rejoined. Press.

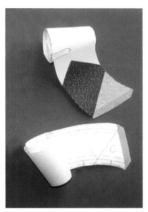

Trim and press.

The first two pieces of a ring are always added in this way. All of the rest of the pieces in the ring are added in the following way. The pieces are added in an alternating sequence.

12. Place the correct fabric piece on the sewing machine extension table with the right side facing up. Position the next solid seam line on the pattern over the fabric with a scant ¼" seam allowance extending beyond the line toward the paper roll that has not yet been pieced. The largest part of this piece will be under the fabric you have already sewn.

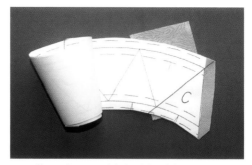

Place the next fabric right side up with the pattern on top.

I always work with the roll that has not been pieced placed in the same position on the sewing machine table. The roll of pattern that has not been pieced is always placed to my left. This seems to help alleviate a few of those common mistakes and allows me to chain piece without getting muddled. On the subject of irritating errors, my teaching experience has shown me that many of the students who have trouble starting off with the foundation piecing are those who insist on continuously checking the back side of the pattern. Just accept the fact that the pieced side of foundation-piecing work can look "wrong" at any time after you first start until the final seam has been sewn. There is a very simple solution to this; don't look. Work on blind faith. I realize that not looking at all is highly unlikely, but don't dwell on the strangeness of it or I guarantee that before long you will be unpicking perfectly good work just because you've managed to convince yourself that "it doesn't look right."

13. Sew this seam in the same way as the first and remove from the machine.
14. Before opening the piece, trim the seam allowance for the seam you have just sewn. It is important to trim the seam allowance to about ¼", not only because it gives a better finish but also because with light-colored fabrics the darker one could show through. If you forget to trim the odd one, it can be trimmed after the paper is removed.
15. Open the piece and finger-press.
16. Trim the fabric even with the edges of the paper and press.
17. Continue to add pieces in this manner until you have completed the ring.
18. Trim the seam allowance of the final piece the same way as the first piece.

19. Using scissors, cut exactly on the curved, dotted cutting line around the outer and inner edges of the ring.

20. To accurately join the ring back into a full circle, insert a straight pin just off the paper through what will become the solid seam lines on the outer and inner curved edges, inserting the pins from the paper side. The pins will be in the seam allowance, protruding at the beginning of the ring. Insert these same pins through the right side of the other end of the ring, making sure that the ring is not twisted. Use a pricking movement until you are able to find and push the pins through in the right place. Push the layers against the pin heads with the pins perpendicular to the seam line.

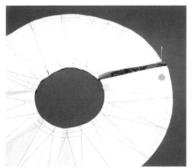

Pin back into a full circle.

21. Pin the layers together to keep them from shifting while stitching the seam. I use three pins for this, placing them at right angles to the seam line. Remove the pins placed in Step 20 and stitch the seam from edge to edge.

Pin the seam.

22. Stitch very close to, but not on, the paper.

23. Trim the seam allowance to a scant ¼" and press to one side. The outer ring is now complete.

Piecing the Inner Ring

The inner ring is made in exactly the same way as the outer ring. Using one of the photocopies, cut out the inner ring section and make this ring following the instructions for the outer ring.

Appliquéing the Center

Appliqué the center onto the ring using your favorite technique. Some of the patterns in the book have large centers, which were all appliquéd, but could be pieced into the ring. I have also seen it done very successfully using fancy machine stitches to appliqué the center. You could also consider using the blind hem method to appliqué by machine or use a satin stitch. I will give hand appliqué methods that work well for me with this type of piecing.

I came up with the following simple, straightforward method for preparing the appliqué center recently when making *Bali Stars*.

1. Lay the piece of fabric you wish to use for the appliqué right side up on a work surface. The fabric really *must* be firmly starched for this to work its very best. Center the paper template for the appliqué circle, face up, on top of the fabric.

2. Machine stitch on the solid seam line using a basting stitch and a contrasting thread.

Place the paper template on top of the right side of the fabric and stitch.

3. Turn it over and trim around the edge of the fabric so roughly ¼" extends beyond the line of stitching to serve as a seam allowance for the appliqué.

4. Press this seam allowance up off the paper toward the center of the circle.

Trim and press.

Be careful to use just the tip of the iron or one of those little irons found in quilt shops nowadays, and move around the circle in small increments. This will help prevent those nasty notches in the edge of the appliqué.

5. **Turn it over so the paper side is on top and use fine-tipped scissors or a seam ripper to snip through the basting stitches. Pull the paper away and you have a lovely circle ready to sew onto your ring.**

I have found this technique works well with a number of shapes for appliqué; not just for circles.

6. **Lay the inner ring flat and place the center on it to check the size. Using a matching thread, sew the prepared center onto the ring.**

Place the center on the inner ring, align, and stitch.

Line up the edge with about three points of the ring, then stitch a little way, line up another point, stitch a bit more, and so on, working around the circle.

I use is a ladder stitch that makes the edge lie very flat. The ladder stitch is achieved by taking ¹⁄₁₆" stitches from the background fabric and immediately when the needle emerges taking an equal stitch in the fold line of the appliqué piece. To avoid a bulging center, be sure to work with the ring flat on a table.

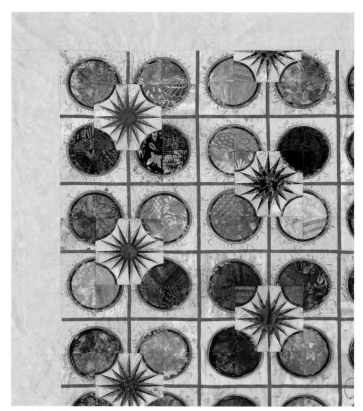

Bali Stars (top details), Barbara Barber, Hampshire, England

Curved Seams

Sewing curves is something many quilters view with trepidation. The very idea used to be enough to put me off even considering any curved design. This continued until I changed my attitude. Now I see a curved seam as a line of stitching made up of many very small straight segments. These straight segments are the areas between the needle and the next pin. I use a lot of pins and the result is a kind of sewing dot-to-dot or in this case, pin-to-pin. This way I need only worry about a very small area at a time.

Outer Curved Seam

This method does not involve clipping the seam allowances at any time.

1. Find and match one of the marks on the background fabric to one of the points on the outside edge of the outer ring, placing right sides together. If appropriate, be sure the ring is orientated correctly within the background. With the paper on top, align the edges and insert a straight pin at a right angle to the curved seam. Do not pin directly through the bulk of the point but about ⅛" to one side of it. Skip the next mark and point. Match and pin the following point, again ⅛" to one side.

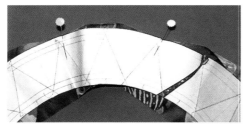

Pin.

2. Now, go back and pin the point between the two pins. Pin ⅛" on each side of this point. Pin the section between the points, placing the pins no more than about ¼" apart.

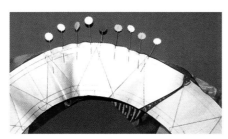

Pin.

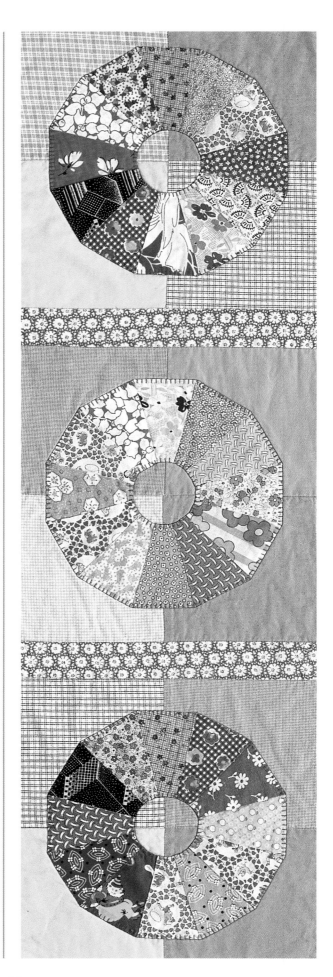

A lot of pins? Yes, but it works and makes sewing the curve foolproof.

3. **Position the edge under the machine so the first stitch falls after the first pin. Lower the needle through the seam line.**

Adjust the fabrics to avoid sewing tucks into the background fabric. Use your thumbs to feel underneath and sort out just the area between the needle and the next pin. Make sure that just that little area is flat. It may seem awkward at first but will soon become second nature.

4. **Stitch using a small stitch setting, paper side up, on the solid seam line, removing each pin just before the needle reaches it.**

If you are new to sewing curves, I suggest that you now stitch the pinned section before pinning any more. Continue to work with short segments, building up the length of stitching as you become more skilled and confident. I think that possibly up to 95% of success with machine quilting is believing it is possible.

Each time you stop to remove a pin, use your thumbs underneath to sort out the fabrics between it and the next pin. You may get a tuck in your first attempts but very quickly this will improve and you will begin to feel confident. It is then that the tucks will be quite rare. This is when you should start pinning and sewing a slightly longer segment, building up the length of the segment point by point as your confidence grows. Soon, the number of pins you have available to use will be the only limiting factor with regard to the length of the curve you sew at one go. There is no need to backstitch these segments.

5. **Pin another section and sew in the same way, overlapping the stitching by about ¼". Do not start and stop on the pieced points because of the bulk of the seams.**
6. **Continue working your way around the circle until it is complete.**

As you go, check the points on the right side to be sure they are sharp. If you find one you don't like the look of, carefully undo about ¼" on each side of the point. Lift or lower the point to correctly position it. Pin and stitch, overlapping the stitches by about ¼" at the beginning and at the end.

7. **After sewing in the entire ring, lay the block flat, right side up, and finger-press the seam. Turn the block over and remove the paper foundation, taking care not to stretch the inside edge of the ring.**

Inner Curved Seam

The pinning and stitching methods are the same as those used for the outer ring. In order to get sharp points on the outer ring, it is very important to make sure the edges are absolutely aligned, especially where there is a point on the outer ring.

The only real difference between sewing the inner and outer curves is the positioning marker. For the outer ring, you mark the background fabric. On the inner ring, the positioning marks are automatically made for you. Look at the paper seam allowance on the outer edge of the inner ring. Between the pieced points of this ring, you will see little "V" shapes. These "V" shapes are the cut-off tips of the pieced points in the outer ring. Therefore, they will serve as the perfect positioning markers.

1. **Match a V-shape to a point in the outer ring, right sides together.**

Match V-shape to point in outer ring.

2. **Pin and sew this curve in the same way as for the outer curve to complete the block.**
3. **Finger-press and then press with an iron, working with the right side on top. Remove all paper foundations.**

1-Ring Circular Piecing

One-Ring Circular Piecing is easy; just follow the 2-Ring Circular Piecing instructions for making the units of the block. The only real difference is that you are using only one ring. Take care to use the correct cutting

line when making the freezer paper template for cutting the hole from the background fabric. If you have any doubts about this review the section on page 24 Understanding the Full-Size Patterns, which is fundamental to success with the whole idea of Really Sharp Piecing. After piecing the ring I still appliqué the center onto the ring before piecing it into the background. Once the center is attached, sew the ring into the prepared background square following instructions for Curved Seams on page 34. After completing the block, press from the top and then remove the foundation paper.

Curved-Unit Piecing

Curved units are sections of curved foundation piecing that run from one edge of a block to another edge of the block. Very often these units are quarter-circles, but they can be a longer string of piecing as in the Solstice block. In fact, this large block has two curved units that help make up the square. The smaller unit is a quarter-circle and the larger one is an oddly shaped unit. They are both pieced in the same way because although they are different shapes they are both curved units that run from one edge of the block to another edge of the same block.

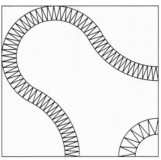

Solstice block

1. **Using a photocopy, cut out the pattern for the curved unit roughly ³⁄₈" larger than the solid seam line on all sides.**

This will be about ⅛" *outside* of the dotted cutting line. If necessary refer to the section in Understanding the Full-Size Patterns that deals with curved unit blocks on page 24.

2. **Piece the curved unit as described in Piecing the Outer Ring on page 29.**

The piecing of a curved unit is exactly the same as for piecing a full ring, except that it does not actually form a full ring. In most cases there will be no need to roll up the pattern, but with longer units it will be easier if you work using the scroll method on page 29.

3. After completing the unit, trim the curved edges exactly on the dotted cutting line. Trim the straight edges as described in Trimming on page 39.

4. Pin and sew the curves the same as described in Curved Seams on page 34.

For me, sewing full-circle curves is always easier than sewing a curved unit to the other pieces of a block. I have found that problems can occur at the beginning and end of the curved seam, sometimes causing the edges of the block to be uneven. To get around these problems, simply do away with the beginning and ending by sewing the first and last ½" of the curved seam. Line up the edges of the first ½" of the seam, right sides together, and pin. Stitch, with the paper on top, on the seam line for ½" and remove from the machine. Bring the other ends of the curved seams together, edges even, and pin. Stitch the last ½" of the curved seam. The seams would, as usual, be sewn with the foundation paper on top. The seam will be sewn in the same way as a circular seam, pressing the seam allowance away from the pieced unit. Sew any remaining curved seams in the block in this way.

5. Remove the foundation papers from the block, leaving a couple intact on any outside edge of the block.

These will not only help to stabilize the block, but will also be helpful in getting sharp points when sewing the block together with other sections of the quilt. I always leave foundations in place on raw edges. If a piece is completely enclosed with finished seams, the foundation paper can be removed.

Non-Circular Blocks

Although these are blocks that have straight edges, they are still made using the ring-piecing techniques. There will be no curved seams and fewer seam allowances shown on the pattern. Although some of the small blocks may have the seam allowance marked on the outside straight edges, the larger ones will not. This is because you will use the rotary cutter to add the ¼" seam allowance when you trim the finished block as detailed in Trimming on page 39. The smaller blocks, which have their seam allowances included, are also trimmed with the rotary cutter. The reason for printing the seam allowances on these small blocks is to indicate clearly that they are full-size patterns.

. . .sewing full-circle curves is always easier than sewing a curved unit to the other pieces of a block.

1. Use one of the photocopies to cut out the block roughly ³⁄₈" larger than the solid seam line on all sides, with the rotary cutter and ruler.

2. Using scissors, cut through the ring exactly on a solid seam line for one of the points.

Do not cut this line on a corner or an angled edge of the block but rather on a straight edge as this will help keep the points that go into the corners or angles really sharp. This is important because the corner is often where the eye first lands when looking at a finished block of this type.

3. Cut out the center, this time cutting about ¹⁄₈" inside of the dashed cutting line. Follow the instructions for Piecing the Outer Ring on page 29, but do not trim the block. Appliqué the center, following instructions for Appliquéing the Center on page 32.

Foundation piecing can be used to add more pieces to these blocks because they have straight edges.

Foundation piece more pieces to these blocks.

If the blocks you are making are not squares, consider whether or not the paper pattern should have the corner bits left on to facilitate foundation piecing these as well after the ring is pieced and joined back into a ring. They could, of course, be added in the normal piecing way but why not do it by foundation piecing when possible?

Pillow cover, 18" x 18", Myra-Jane Ibbetson, Dorset, England

Foolproof Curves

Straight-Unit Piecing

The patterns for straight units are all printed without seam allowances. These units will be trimmed, as detailed in Trimming, to include a ¼" seam allowance after the unit is completely pieced. Cut out the pattern roughly ⅝" larger than the solid seam line on all sides using the rotary cutter and straightedge.

For long units glue or tape photocopies together to form the pattern. Always overlap by a square or triangle section in order to ensure a straight edge for the length of the unit. At times it will be necessary to cut off part of a photocopied pattern in order to get the correct pattern configuration. When this happens, be sure to cut roughly ⅝" beyond the final, solid seam line required for the pattern. On long units, it is extremely important to check and double check that you have glued your foundation pattern together correctly.

The piecing of a straight unit, long or short, is the same as used in Piecing the Outer Ring, on page 29, except that you are making a straight unit and do not cut into or join into a ring. Remember to piece long units using the scroll method, though this will not be necessary for short units.

Trimming

Almost all of the straight-edged patterns in the book do not have the seam allowance included on the pattern. Use a rotary cutter and ruler to very accurately add and trim the ¼" seam allowance at the same time. The method is the same whether it is a block or a straight unit and whether or not the seam allowances were printed on the pattern. Add the seam allowance to each side as you cut by positioning the ¼" line of the ruler to the solid seam line of the block or unit. Always check the placement of the ruler several times, up and down the seam, before cutting. Check this placement again after you have applied pressure on the ruler, as the paper makes the ruler much more likely to slip. When trimming a unit that is longer than the straightedge, simply position the ruler on a segment of the unit, about 15" at a time, and trim. Move the unit along on the cutting board and position the ruler and trim another section of the unit. To ensure a straight edge on long units, be sure to overlap by placing the ruler on part of the previously cut section.

A Fishy Affair

A Fishy Affair, 86½'' x 86½'', Barbara Barber, Hampshire, England

Foolproof Curves

I love this quilt! It was built around the two fish fabrics. I adore scrap quilts and other than the fish fabrics, all of the fabrics were taken from my stash. I've always found that scrap quilts are a good formula for those quilters who are less than sure about their color choices, since it simply can't go wrong, looks far more difficult than it is, and soon gives them the confidence to deal with color in more challenging ways. Pick one or two fabrics to feature and then simply keep adding to them, the more the merrier.

The main block is 18" x 18" and was taken from my quilt, *Solstice*, page 45. In *Solstice*, this block was a 6" square.

Materials

- **Black Fish Print:** 1¼ yards for background of 4 blocks

- **Turquoise Fish Print:** 1⅔ yards for background of 5 blocks

- **Green, Orange, and Turquoise Prints:** ¾ yard each of 9 different fabrics for blocks and borders

- **Yellow Prints:** ⅞ yard each of 9 different fabrics for blocks, borders, and 4 small sashing blocks

- **Red, Black, and Blue Multicolored Prints:** ½ yard each of 9 different fabrics for blocks, sashing squares, and 4 small sashing blocks

- 3⅛ yard lengthwise stripe

- 7⅝ yards for backing

- ⅞ yard black print for binding

- 90" x 90" batting

- Freezer paper

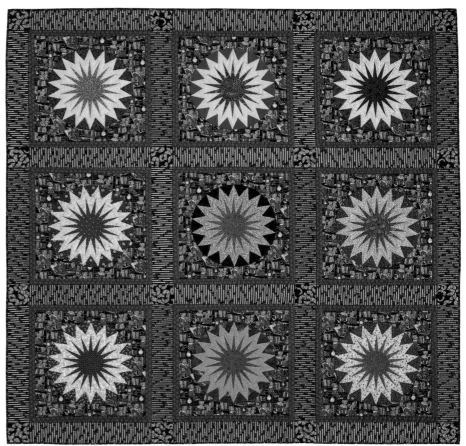

Geoff & The Bears, 74" x 74", Barbara Barber, Hampshire, England. Here is another variation that would be a good choice if you wanted a slightly smaller quilt.

Detail of *A Fishy Affair*

A Fishy Affair

Photocopies

- 19 copies of Really Sharp Piecing design, on pullout
- 5 copies of *A Fishy Affair* sashing block, page 44
- 18 copies of *A Fishy Affair* Section 1, on pullout
- 18 copies of *A Fishy Affair* Section 2, on pullout
- Copies of *A Fishy Affair* Sections 1 and 2 as required to make border foundations

Cutting

Black Fish Print
- Cut 4 squares 18½" x 18½" for the background of 4 of the blocks.

Turquoise Fish Print
- Cut 5 squares 18½" x 18½" for the background of 5 of the blocks.

Green, Orange, and Turquoise Prints
- Cut 2 strips 2½" wide from each of the 9 prints. From these strips, cut 18 rectangles 2½" x 3¼" from each fabric for D.
- Cut 5 strips 3½" wide from each of the 9 prints. From these strips, cut 64 rectangles 3½" x 2¾" from each fabric for E (blocks and triangles on outer edges of border).

Yellow Prints
- Cut 1 strip 4" wide from each of the 9 prints. From these strips, cut 18 rectangles 4" x 2⅝" from each fabric for B.
- Cut 1 strip 3¼" wide from each of the 9 prints. From these strips, cut 18 rectangles 3¼" x 2⅝" from each fabric for C.
- Cut 5 strips 3½" wide from each of the 9 prints. From these strips, cut 60 rectangles 3½" x 2¾" from each fabric for F for blocks and inner triangles in border.

- Cut 1 strip 3" wide from 4 of the prints. From these strips, cut 16 rectangles 3" x 1¾" from each fabric for H for sashing blocks.

Red, Black, and Blue Multicolored Prints
- Cut 2 strips 1¾" wide from each of the 9 prints. From these strips, cut 18 rectangles 1¾" x 4" from each fabric for A.
- Cut 1 square 5" x 5" from each of the 9 prints for the block appliquéd centers.
- Cut 12 squares total 4½" x 4½" from a variety of the 9 prints for sashing squares.
- Cut 1 strip 3" wide from 4 of the prints. From these strips, cut 16 rectangles 3" x 1⅜" from each fabric for G in sashing blocks.
- Cut 1 square 2¾" x 2¾" from each of the same 4 prints used above for appliquéd centers for sashing blocks.

Stripe
- Cut 24 crosswise strips 4½" x 22½".

Block Construction

1. Make 9 Really Sharp Piecing blocks using the 18½" x 18½" squares for the background of the blocks and the pieces cut for the A, B, C, and D pieces. Use the 5" x 5" squares for the appliquéd centers. Refer to 2-Ring Circular Piecing on page 28.

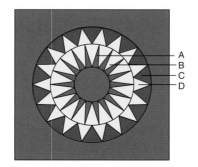

2. Using the pieces cut for E and F, make 18 each of *A Fishy Affair* Section 1 and *A Fishy Affair* Section 2. Refer to Straight-Unit Piecing on page 39. Trim each of the units following the instructions for Trimming on page 39.

Make 18 of each.

3. Make 4 small sashing blocks using copies of the Sashing Block. Refer to Non-Circular Blocks on page 37. Use the pieces cut for G and H and the 2¾" x 2¾" square for the appliquéd center. Trim the outer edges of the blocks, referring to Trimming on page 39.

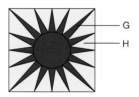

Quilt Top Construction

1. Sew one of the shorter units (Section 1) to the top and one to the bottom of each of the blocks made in Step 1 above. Add a longer pieced unit (Section 2) to each side of each of the blocks. Press the seam allowances toward the block.

Make 9.

2. Arrange the blocks, sashing strips, sashing squares, and sashing blocks. Sew into rows, pressing the seams toward the sashing strips as you go.

3. Sew the rows together to form the center of the quilt. Press the seams to one side. Remove the foundation papers from the blocks, sashing square blocks, and triangle units.

4. Prepare the paper foundations for the pieced border by gluing together copies of *A Fishy Affair* sections 1 and 2. To ensure accuracy, overlap the units by one whole triangle when gluing or taping the copies together. For more information about gluing photocopied design together see page 23. When preparing foundation papers for a long string of piecing, I find it very helpful to number the individual units. By writing directly on the foundations, I am certain to end up with the correct size strip that has the correct number of pieces.

Quilt Top Construction

Make 2 of each.

5. Use the pieces cut from the 9 different prints in green, orange, and turquoise at random for the outer triangles in the border sections and the pieces cut from the different yellows for the inner triangles in the border. Piece the border, referring to Straight-Unit Piecing on page 39. Trim the borders as described in Trimming on page 39.

6. Add one of the shorter border sections to the top and one to the bottom of the quilt. Find and match centers. Pin and stitch. Stitch with the pieced borders on top, using the seam line on the paper as a guide. Press the seam allowances toward the sashing.

7. Sew the longer border sections to each side of the quilt (see Step 6).

Finishing

1. Leave the papers intact on the outer edges until just before layering the quilt to prevent the pieced section from stretching out of shape. Just before layering the top with the batting and backing, carefully remove the paper foundations from the pieced borders. Layer the quilt top, batting, and backing. Pin or baste.

2. Quilt the seams in the ditch and the sashing between each stripe on the fabric. Free-motion quilt the background of the blocks in a wave formation to carry out the theme of the fish fabrics.

3. Bind the edges with 2"-wide bias binding cut from a 28" x 28" square and add a label.

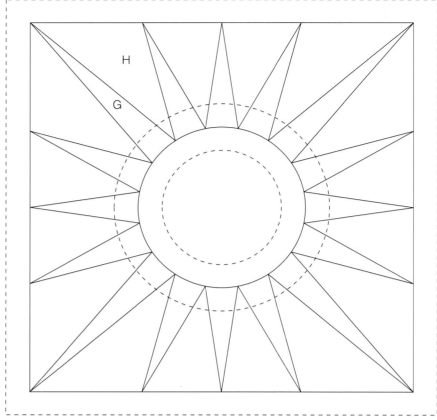

A Fishy Affair Sashing Block

Solstice

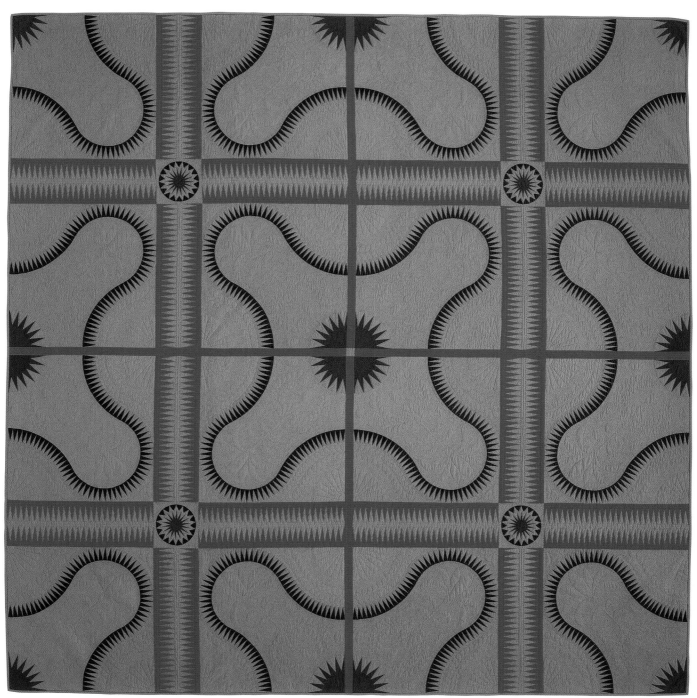

Solstice, 102" x 102", Barbara Barber, Hampshire, England

Solstice was a dream come true for me. I say that here in such a bold fashion not to impress you with the quilt but to get across the important role I feel mental attitude plays in our quilting achievements. I adore reading the state heritage books that many of the individual states have produced and I urge you, to try reading some of them. Try it! Those women completed magnificent quilts, often made from so very little under such difficult circumstances. More than anything, those ladies of the past gave me the courage to believe it was possible.

Materials

- **Blue Solid:** 1 yard
- **Red Solid:** 4⅜ yards
- **Green Solid:** 2⅞ yards
- **Orange Solid:** 17¼ yards
- 9⅛ yards for backing
- 1 yard for binding
- 106" x 106" batting
- Freezer paper

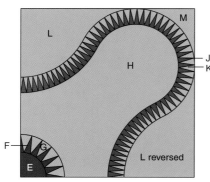
Solstice block

Photocopies

- 9 copies of *Solstice* sashing block, page 51
- 32 copies of Solstice sashing unit, on pullout, enlarge 200%.

- 16 copies of F/G Curved unit (found within Solstice block on pullout)
- Copies as required of E, H, L, L reversed, and M pieces for making templates (found within Solstice block on pullout)
- 1 copy of Solstice block to use for the quilting design on pullout, enlarge 200%

NOTE: The Solstice block is a large pattern, on pullout. The quilting design is an important part of this quilt and is included on the block pattern, which contains the piecing pattern. During piecing, ignore the quilting design lines on the pattern. Refer to the drawings below as you prepare to cut your photocopies for piecing.

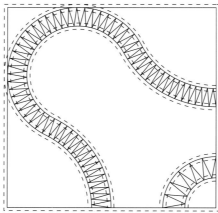
Piecing pattern with all seam lines and cutting lines

Quilting design as it would look without any of the cutting lines

Cutting

Blue Solid

- Cut 2 strips 2" wide. From these strips, cut 72 rectangles 2" x 1" for A in the 4 small sashing blocks.
- Cut 4 squares 2½" x 2 ½" for the appliquéd centers in the 4 small sashing blocks.
- Cut 5 strips 3½" wide. From these strips, cut 112 rectangles 3½" x 1¾" for F in the large blocks.
- Cut 2 strips 4¼" wide. Refer to Photocopied Templates on page 27. Using photocopies, cut 16 E pieces.

Red Solid

NOTE: Cut the 50½" long strips from the lengthwise grain of the fabric first.

- Cut 4 strips 2" x 50½". These strips form the red cross through the center of the quilt.
- Cut 32 strips 1¼" x 22 ⅛" for the sashing.
- Cut 34 strips 3" wide. From these strips, cut 928 rectangles 3" x 1¼" for the red triangles in the sashing units.

Green Solid

- Cut 3 strips 1¼" wide. From these strips, cut 72 rectangles 1¼" x 1¾" for D in the 4 small sashing blocks.
- Cut 25 strips 3" wide. From these strips, cut 1,024 rectangles 3" x 1" for J.

Orange Solid

- Cut 16 strips 1¼" x 22⅛" for the sashing.
- Cut 2 strips 2" wide. From these strips, cut 72 rectangles 2" x 1" for B.
- Cut 3 strips 1¼" wide. From these strips, cut 72 rectangles 1¼" x 1¾" for C.

- Cut 4 squares 7¼" x 7¼" for the background of the 4 small sashing blocks.

- Cut 6 strips 3½" wide. From these strips, cut 96 rectangles 3½" x 2¼" for G.

- Cut 32 strips 3" wide. From these strips, cut 1,040 rectangles 3" x 1¾" for K.

- Cut 27 strips 3" wide. From these strips, cut 864 rectangles 3" x 1½" for the orange triangles in the sashing units.

- Cut 16 pieces for each of H, L, L reversed, and M. Refer to Photocopied Templates on page 27. Use the freezer-paper method to make templates for these large pieces. Remember to mark placement points on all of the curved fabric edges in order to match them with the foundation units when sewing them together.

- Cut 1 square 2" x 2" for the square in the center of the quilt.

Block Construction

1. Using the 7¼" x 7¼" orange background squares, the 2½" x 2½" blue squares for the appliquéd centers, and the pieces cut for the A, B, C, and D pieces, make 4 Solstice sashing blocks. Refer to 2-Ring Piecing on page 28. Although this is a small block, it can be sewn together in the usual way, using your sewing machine. However, for ease, you may wish to consider hand appliqué as an alternative when joining the inner ring unit to the outer ring unit. This should be done after sewing the outer ring into the background square by machine and after you have appliquéd the center onto the inner ring.

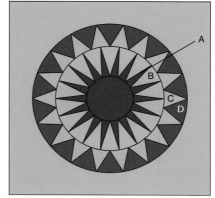

Sashing block

2. The large blocks are pieced using the Curved Unit method on page 36. In this block there are two curved units, a large one and a small one. Although there are two curved units within the block, you still put the block together in the same way as a block with a single curved unit. As you add pieces to the curved units, be sure to match points along the curves and pin well. For all the curved seams throughout the block, press the seam allowances away from the foundation curved unit.

3. Piece the F/G units using the blue and orange pieces. Alternate blue and orange pieces, starting and ending with a blue piece. Add the E piece to this unit.

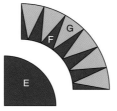

Add E to F/G.

4. Sew this unit to the H piece.

Sew E/F/G to H.

5. Piece the J/K units using the orange and green pieces. Alternate orange and green pieces, starting and ending with an orange piece.

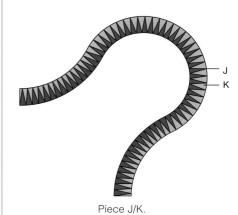

Piece J/K.

6. Sew this J/K unit to the H piece.

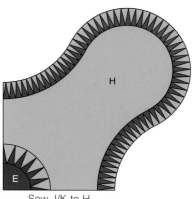

Sew J/K to H.

7. Add an L piece to one side and the L reversed piece to the other side of the unit. Add the M piece to complete the block.

Sashing Construction

1. Using the photocopies of Solstice sashing unit, make 32 units. Refer to Straight-Unit Piecing on page 39. Alternate red and orange pieces, starting and ending with a red piece. Trim all of these sashing units as described in Trimming on page 39.

Make 32.

2. Sew a 1¼" x 22⅛" red sashing strip to each of these sashing units, being sure to attach the red strip to the side of the unit that is edged with red triangles. Find and match the centers and pin together carefully. Stitch with the paper foundation on top, using the line as a stitching guide to keep the points really sharp. Press the seam toward the red strip. Sew a 1¼" x 22⅛" orange sashing strip to the other side of half of the sashing units. Press the seam toward the orange strip. Sew the remaining sashing units to the free edge of the orange strip, pressing the seam toward the orange.

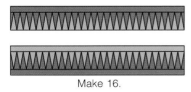

Make 16.

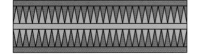

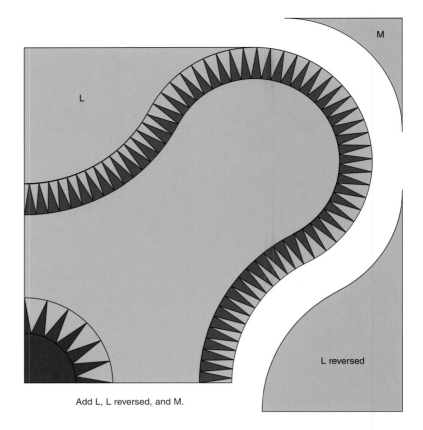

Add L, L reversed, and M.

3. Remove all of the paper foundations from the sashing units except for the last 2 or 3 triangles at each end of the foundations. The paper triangles that are left intact will be helpful in keeping those points sharp when sewing the sashing units together with the sashing squares.

4. Sew 1 block to each side of 8 of the sashing units. Find and match the centers and pin carefully. Stitch with the block uppermost, using the foundation line as a guide in the area where the curved unit touches the sashing. Press the seam toward the sashing unit.

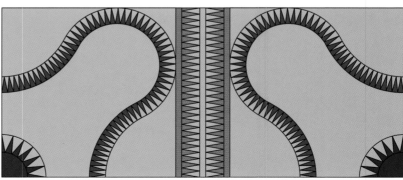

Sew one block to each side of sashing.

5. Sew a sashing unit to both sides of the four sashing blocks. Stitch with the sashing unit uppermost and press the seam toward the sashing.

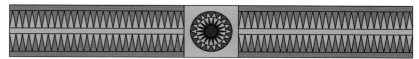

Sew sashing units to sashing blocks.

Quilt Top Construction

1. Sew one of the units made in Step 5 to each side of the units made in Step 4. Press the seam toward the sashing.

2. Lay out the prepared units with the red strips and the orange center square. Stitch together as shown. Remove any remaining foundation papers.

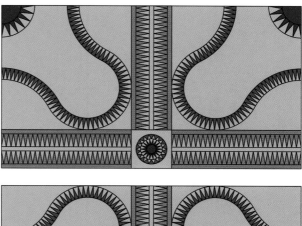

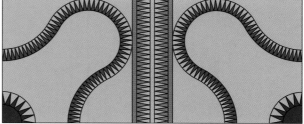

Block construction

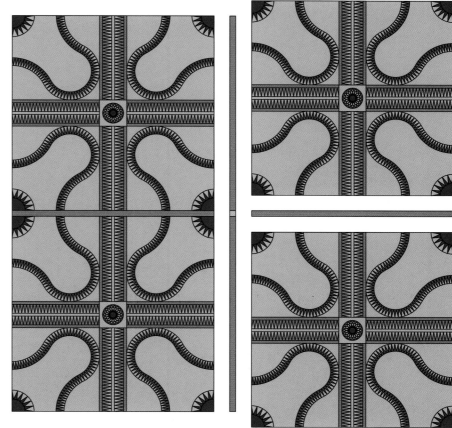

Quilt Top Construction

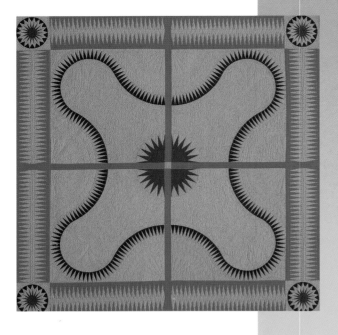

Finishing

1. Mark the quilt top using the quilting design printed on the Solstice block pattern. This can be done easily with a light box. If the fabric is very light colored, you may be able to simply trace the design through the fabric without the aid of a light box. This will be made easier if you darken the lines on the copy of the quilting design with a permanent black felt tip marker. All seams of Solstice were quilted and then the background was stipple quilted.

2. Layer the quilt top, batting, and backing. Pin or baste.

3. Quilt as marked.

4. Bind the edges with 2"-wide bias binding cut from a 30" x 30" square of orange fabric and add a label.

My husband made me a splendid light box and I really would hate to be without it, as it is invaluable for marking quilting designs on my quilt tops, as well as for appliqué. It is large and not very pretty but it does the job intended better than any of the commercial light boxes I have seen. Peter made it from a double-glazed door panel that measured 26" x 34". He made a timber box that is 6" deep and fitted the glass panel into the top of it. There are two fluorescent light units fitted in the bottom of it. He also gave me the luxury of a switch so that I do not have to unplug it each time I finish using it. The finished box is very heavy but the glass panel can be easily removed and the bottom moved separately. I hope this gives you some idea if you are thinking of having one made.

Solstice Sashing Block
full size

Originality Free-For-All

In previous chapters, you have seen many ways to use ring piecing combined with spikes to produce some very dramatic results. I cannot urge you enough to start making those rough drawings! In this chapter, I want you to go in some brand new directions I have developed to make fun, quick quilts. I've always felt certain that if you wish to undertake the extra effort required to develop one of these techniques through your own imagination and originality that you can come up with a truly scrumptious quilt that is unique to you and you alone.

An example of this can be seen in my quilt *Twinkle Toes*. The border was the starting point and consists of very straightforward foundation-pieced blocks. The central part of the quilt was much more complex and not so easy to piece using some very complex blocks by Jenny Beyer. However, the merit of the extra time invested in what started as quick, simple border blocks was rewarded when it was named Champion Quilt, Quilts UK 1993.

I'm not saying there is anything wrong with sticking with the formula of simple, quick, fun quilts and I know for a start that I shall never stop making them. There is something very soothing about mindless sewing. On the other hand, don't be afraid to let your own personality shine through, you do not have to make a carbon copy of anyone's quilt. You can make your own and let yourself show through. A prime example of this is *Kaleidoscope*, page 64. The center is a very good example of how my piecing system really does work. The finished quilt is stunning and became an award winner at the National Patchwork Championships 1998, London.

With the following three quilts, I have not given full instructions for the quilts but rather a method to help you make an original design using these techniques. As you read through this chapter, think "quick, quality quilts you can give away, if you can bear to do so, without giving away half your life." On the other hand, as you see these fun ideas with Ring Piecing, don't be afraid to accept different answers when you ask "What if?"

Twinkle Toes, 108'' x 108'', Barbara Barber, Hampshire, England. Collection of Clive and Pat Dunning, Hampshire, England

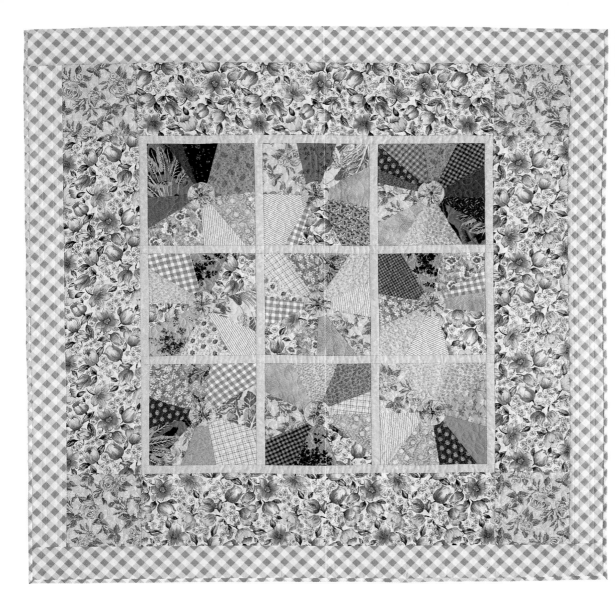

Ethel Mertz,
64'' x 64'', Linda Park,
Westborough,
Massachusetts

Free-Form Ring Piecing

When I first made my Flannel Fun quilt, I used large 15" blocks in order to achieve a full-size quilt quickly for a Christmas present. (It is not pictured here because my daughter loves it and the dear thing is very nearly worn out!) I have since fallen in love with making a 6" version that is also made in flannel and ever so sweet. This is a quilt that works well in either flannel or cotton.

My friend Linda Park teaches this class the way I feel it should be taught, which is to say, "Make your squares any size you like." You see, she had already discovered for herself the joys of working as the mood takes you. Linda made *Ethel Mertz* as a teaching sample for her class. It is made with cotton fabrics, most of which, according to Linda, "would make the perfect dress for Ethel."

Ethel Mertz

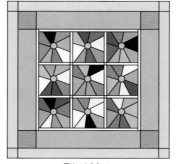

Ethel Mertz

The blocks can be any size you like. In this quilt they are 12" square with a 1" sashing. There are two borders: the first, floral border is 8" wide and the outer, check border is 4" wide. The blocks are made using the techniques on page 37, Non-Circular Blocks. The big difference here is that you will not be using photocopied patterns, but will instead be drawing your own as you go. For quilters who are wary of their creative initiative this can be a first step in originating your own work and will help give confidence and free up even the most timid of "closet designers."

1. Use a ruler to draw a square on paper that measures the size you want your finished block to be. Cut out the square, leaving approximately 3/8" of extra paper beyond the square for seam allowances. Draw a circle in the center. The size of this circle is entirely your choice and can be drawn freehand, as accuracy is not important here. The hole will be covered with an appliqué patch.

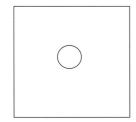

Draw a square, cut it out, then draw a circle in the center.

2. Using a ruler, draw lines from the outer edges of the square into the center circle. The number of pieces you make in the block is up to you.

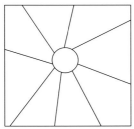

Draw lines from outer edges to circle.

3. Make the blocks, referring to the information about Non-Circular Blocks on page 37. Trim the blocks, referring to Trimming on page 39. Cover the center hole with a piece of appliqué of your choice.

Linda chose to use the yo-yos, since she feels they add a nice touch of texture and can also provide a portable project. She adores these little things and obviously, she's not alone, since most of these quilts tend to end up with a yo-yo in the middle. Other shapes such as hearts or circles could be cut from fabric and attached to the block with a buttonhole stitch.

If you choose to use a decorative machine stitch, try a sample using a thread color that you fancy. I have found that a contrasting 30-weight appliqué thread works best with the decorative buttonhole-type stitches; while I would probably use a thinner, matching thread if using a straight stitch. Be sure to test the stitch first, since you may wish to change the settings that are preset in your machine. I make my buttonhole stitch length a bit shorter and wider for this type of work. It makes me feel more secure about it staying put. Be sure to secure the ends with about 1/4" of tiny straight stitches at the beginning and end of the fancy stitches.

Detail of *Ethel Mertz*

4. After making the number of blocks you require, put the rest of the quilt together in the normal fashion, remove the paper, and quilt to finish.

Appli-Quilt Ring Piecing

When I came up with this method, I started a long chain of ideas which, in part, provided the springboard for the techniques in Part II of this book. I feel confident this method is an ongoing process. When making my *Really Quick Quilts* video, I asked Julie Standen if she'd be interested in making this quilt. Julie agreed, with the understanding that time was restricted due to her work. I agreed happily because I knew this was perfect; what better way to demonstrate the ease and speed of a quick quilt than by having a career woman make it? The entire quilt was finished within two weeks and that, by any standard, is fast! I gave Julie a drawing for the appliquéd plate and verbal instructions.

As you read about this quilt, please understand, it does work and is easy. In fact, there is something mischievously fun, almost daring, since it goes against the norm but still gives a quality finish. I hope as you read you will open your mind to other shapes that can be given this treatment, as well as new settings for them. Mind you, I don't blame you if you still go ahead and make a quilt exactly like *Flirty Thirties*, it's definitely on my list of quilts I need to make!

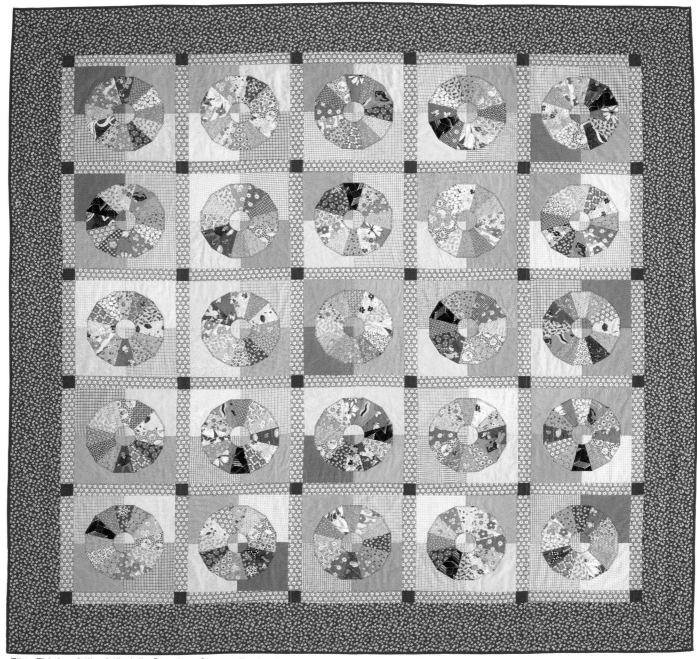

Flirty Thirties, 84" x 84", Julie Standen, Clutton, England

Flirty Thirties

1. Use photocopies of the *Flirty Thirties* pattern, page 57, to make this quilt, enlarging it to suit the size block you wish to make.

The finished block size is 12". The four-patch design within the block is composed of 6" squares. The sashing is 2" wide with a 6" border around the outside of the quilt. A quilt made using these dimensions and 25 blocks will finish at 84" square.

2. Make the ring-piecing units following the information given on page 37. The difference is that these pieced rings are being prepared for appliqué and will have a turned-under edge on the inner and outer edge of the ring.

The piecing differs from other ring piecing in these points:

- Cut the ring pattern out exactly on the outer and inner solid lines.

- When cutting and piecing, be aware that you must leave excess fabric extending beyond the paper at outer and inner edges to be turned under as seam allowances.

- Do not stitch off the edge of the paper pattern but do backstitch at both ends to secure.

- After re-joining the ring to form a circle, carefully turn under and press in the seam allowances that extend beyond the paper. Use the paper as a template to gently press the seam allowances up and over the ring.

- DO NOT remove any of the papers yet and put the pieced rings to one side.

3. **Make your quilt top in the normal way but DO NOT attach the pieced rings.**

When you have finished the top you should have what looks like a quilt composed of four-patch blocks.

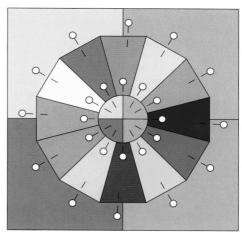

Pin in position.

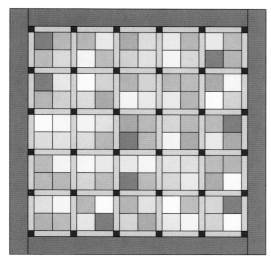

Quilt Top

4. **Layer the quilt top, batting, and backing. Pin or baste.**
5. **Quilt the straight seams in-the-ditch.**
6. **Bind the edges.**
7. **Give the paper-pieced ring another good press to keep the seam allowance turned under before carefully removing the paper. Work with one at a time, completing each before removing the paper from the next. Center it, right side up, on one of the pieced blocks in the quilt and pin in position, using plenty of straight pins to hold it and prevent movement.**

Here again, as in Step 3 of *Ethel Mertz*, page 55, I like to use a buttonhole or other fancy machine stitch to appliqué the center. Also, start and stop the "appli-quilt" stitching with about ¼" of tiny straight stitches to secure the threads.

8. **Continue adding rings to the quilt until you're finished and if your mind starts to wander, you can be planning your next quilt!**

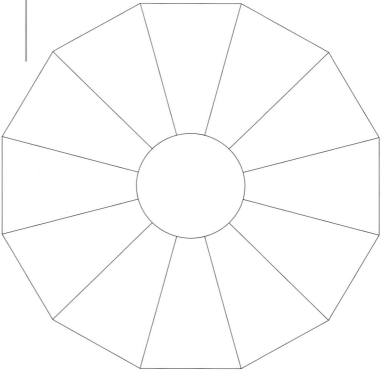

Flirty Thirties: Although this is a pattern, you can print it any size you decide. See Step 1, page 56.

My Stars

Teaching has allowed me to meet thousands of wonderful people all over the world who have become both friends and inspirations to me through my quilting life. *Summer Cats* is an example of this inspiration, because it was through asking a student if she would like to make this quilt for my video that I had the privilege to become friends with one of the world's best people! I gave her a very vague description of the effect I was after as far as the stars were concerned and she came up with the wonderful block in that quilt.

Detail of *Summer Cats* by Veronica Gilbert, Birmingham, England

Stars made using this particular technique come out like the stars in nature; no two are exactly alike. This is another "make up your own block design" but this time I am going to take you further to include a free-form border as well. Just let go and have fun, that's what this is all about!

Sloppy Stars

The week before I was due to film my *Really Quick Quilts* video, the producer came to review what precisely we were going to do. When he arrived, we went through the various quilts that were to be covered. Then I showed him a heap of fabrics on the table and said that these were going to be used for making the final quilt for the video. The only comment he made was that they were "very colorful" and then asked to see the

finished example. I stuttered a bit and reassured him that by next week that heap would become a quilt. A dubious producer left that day and returned a week later to find my quilt completed. Amazed, he said that we would truly be working on quick quilts and because he was so impressed he gave this quilt, *Sloppy Stars*, a starring role in the video.

This quilt is composed of 9 blocks that are 12" square (finished size). They are set, on point, in a larger block with the use of corner triangles. When designing your own quilts certain measurements are very handy to keep to mind and the following is one that I have used so much over the years that I no longer have to look it up. I urge you, when drafting or designing, to keep Nancy Johnson-Srebro's book, *Measure the Possibilities*, handy for reference. It has endless gems of information for doing design work.

To find the diagonal measurement of a square or allow you to know what size a quilt will finish if you should set your blocks on point, use the following formulas.

To find the diagonal measurement of a square, multiply the size of the square by 1.414. For *Sloppy Stars*, I used 12" squares that, when multiplied by 1.414, equaled 16.968. This was rounded up to 17.

Sloppy Stars, 80½" x 80½", Barbara Barber, Hampshire, England

Foolproof Curves

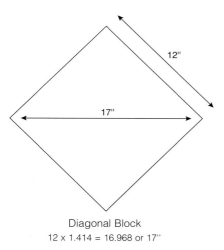

Diagonal Block
12 x 1.414 = 16.968 or 17"

Likewise, if you have a diagonal measurement and wish to figure out the size square required in order to add corner triangles cut from bias squares, the number is the same but this time you are dividing instead of multiplying. For the star block of *Sloppy Stars*, the 12" square is divided by 1.414, giving a sum of 8.4865629. This is near enough to be rounded up to 8½". The amount to add for seam allowance is ⅞", plus the measurement of the square.

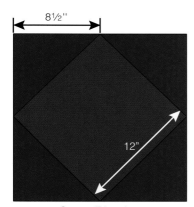

Corner Triangles
12 ÷ 1.414 = 8.4865629 or 8½"

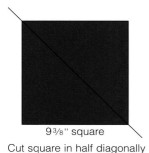

9⅜" square

Cut square in half diagonally
for corner triangles

In this case, the square would measure 8½" plus ⅞", meaning you would need to cut a 9⅜" square and then cut it in half once on the diagonal. This will give you triangles of the correct size to add on to the star blocks when set on point.

The measurements for the rest of the quilt are straightforward. The strip that runs around the star block is ½" wide. Sashing strips were made 3" wide. The unpieced border is 4" wide and the jagged outer border is 6" wide (finished sizes).

Even if you wish to make this quilt without altering the design to any extent, you can very easily change the size of the finished quilt by simply enlarging or reducing the star block. By using a 10" star block in place of the 12" one, the size will reduce significantly from 80" to 71" square. If you are unsure about working out quilt measurements, it would be quite a useful exercise to work through the measurements using a 10" block to come up with a 71" square. Becoming confident in figuring out sizes was a major step forward for me, as a beginner, toward designing my own quilts. For a start, it can begin to undo some of what is for most of us quilters, an almost ingrained phobia of numbers in any form connected with quilts! I have learned to deal with my math-in-quilts phobia in the way that some experts suggest dealing with other phobias, by exposure! The answer is to make friends with a good calculator.

1. **To make the star blocks, you must first design and draw your pattern—that's the fun part! First, draw a square of the size you wish your finished block to be. Put your pencil down on one of the lines and, using a ruler, draw lines from one edge to the other, working around the square to form a star.**

You can make the stars as uniform or as way-out as you fancy. If you look at *Sloppy Stars*, you will see that one or two of them, if seen in isolation, are hardly recognizable as stars. When seen with the group of stars, I like to think in terms of "variety is the spice of life." When I was doing mine, I simply drew a star of the sort that I thought was ever so clever when I was about 6 years old.

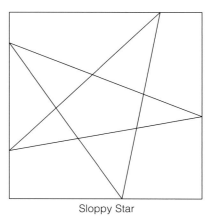

Sloppy Star

2. Make the blocks referring to Non-Circular Blocks, page 37. In *Sloppy Stars* I used a decorative stitch to attach the appliquéd centers with a matching thread.

The angular shape of the center was retained in *Sloppy Stars* but by looking at the block shown of *Summer Cats*, page 58, you can see how effective a circle can be as well.

3. Square up the blocks following the instructions in Trimming, page 39. DO NOT remove the paper pattern until the quilt top is completed.
4. Put the center of the quilt together and add the 4"-wide plain border.
5. Make your own pattern for the jagged border. Start by drawing the section full size onto paper for piecing. You then have the choice of drawing the whole thing before starting to sew or by drawing each line as you come to it.

When I pieced the first border, I drew it all out before sewing any of it, but as I advanced I discovered that it was easier to work one bit at a time with the drawing as well as the piecing.

6. Paper piece the jagged border following the instructions for Straight-Unit Piecing and Trimming on page 39.
7. Sew these borders onto the edges to complete the top.
8. Remove the paper from the center section of the quilt but leave the paper in the outer borders until you absolutely have to remove them. I use this technique for any quilt that has foundation-pieced borders.
9. Layer the quilt for pinning or basting, leaving the edges free. After pinning the center, fold back the paper-lined borders flat onto the body of the quilt and carefully remove the paper.
10. Quilt as desired and add the binding. You should, of course, also add a label and you will probably wish to name the quilt as well.

Detail of *Sloppy Stars*

Foolproof Curves

Gallery

Goato & Friends
83″ x 83″, Barbara Barber
Hampshire, England.
Collection of the Museum
of the American Quilter's Society
Paducah, Kentucky

Meridian
80" x 80"
Shelagh Jarvis
London, England

**Rolled'em,
Rolled'em,
Rolled'em
Too Far**
69" x 94"
Myra-Jane Ibbetson
Dorset, England

Good Morning Sunshine

108'' x 108''
Phoebe Bartleet
Hampshire, England

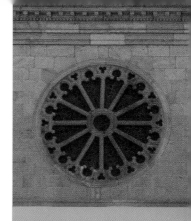

PH Balance
85" x 85"
Marcia J. Katz,
Valley Village
California

Kaleidoscope
100" x 100"
Sarah Hadfield
Nottinghamshire
England

Hexstar
69" x 75"
Julie Standen
Bristol, England

Lilac Feathers
90" x 90"
Barbara Barber
Hampshire, England

Columns
90" x 90"
Barbara Barber
Hampshire, England.
Collection of Colin
and Marilyn Currill
Oxford, England

Azdaz
78" x 78"
Lois Andrews
Surrey, England

Pumpkin Pie
79½" x 79½"
Linda Park
Westborough, Massachusetts

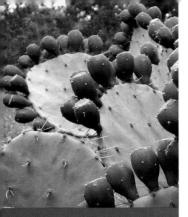

Bette's Pastel Sunburst
85" x 85"
Anne Ray
Lambourne,
Berkshire, England

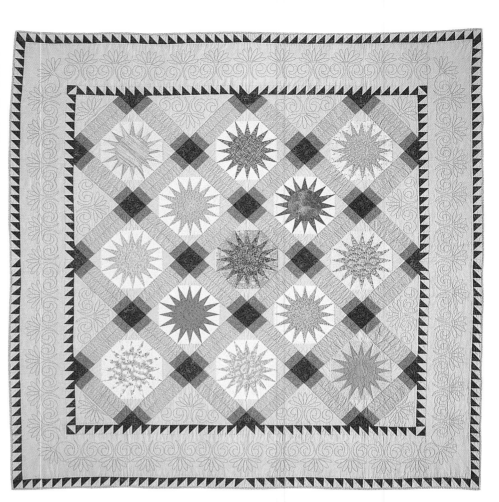

Leap Frog
76" x 76"
Cathy A. Tongue
Reading,
Pennsylvania

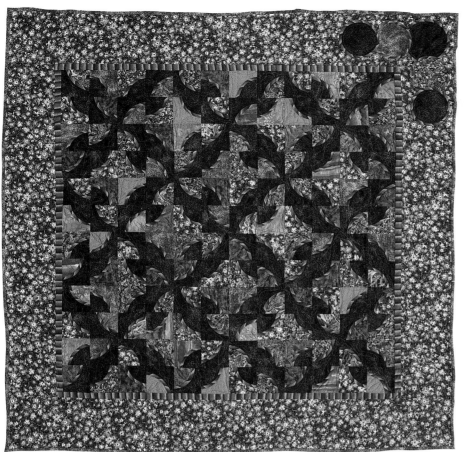

Leading Up the Garden Path
62" x 62"
Julia Barker
Devon, England

Dots Out Back
74" x 74"
Janet Benjafield
Devon, England

**Expanding
Universe**
100" x 100"
Myra-Jane Ibbetson
Dorset, England

Foolproof Curves

Across the Pond
76" x 76"
Janet Benjafield
Devon, England

Wild Thing
74½" x 74½"
Anne E. McLain
Douglassville,
Pennsylvania

Part II

Bias Strips

Create curved piecing using bias strips.

New Ideas and New Techniques

Curved Piecing Without Sewing Curved Seams

This technique uses bias binding within the design area of the quilt top rather than just as a decorative finish along the outside edges of a quilt. With that in mind, I suppose it should be called *bias edging or bias strips* here and throughout the rest of this book, but old habits die hard and I think most people, myself included, would be just as happy to simply refer to it as *bias binding*.

Think of any technique or combination of techniques that can be applied or laid onto a fabric, in other words, appliquéd. The appliqué used in this book is the most straightforward you'll ever do and I promise you will not even think of it as appliqué. The bias binding, which likewise you won't consider as such, is used to give the impression of intricate or curved piecing and at the same time provides a method for securing the appliqué while tidying the edges and achieving some of the quilting.

If you are one who has firmly believed that you cannot and therefore will not ever produce your own original, high-quality designs, then I really do wish I could somehow convince you to actually do the design exercises. Don't simply read and think, "Oh, that's a good idea," or "Yes, I can see how that would work." After you read, take your pencil and make those rough sketches! At first, it will probably feel awkward, but that downside is nothing compared to the high of actually *feeling* your design muscles working—it's wonderful!

This technique creates the look of curved piecing without sewing curved seams. Instead, you topstitch curved pieces to a background and cover the rough edge with bias edging. The bias edge is stitched down in the quilting, so it does not require traditional machine or hand appliqué!

1. Create a design with a wavy strip, arc, or circle.

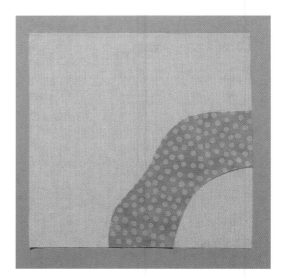

2. Position the design on the background. Lay the raw edges of prepared bias edging even with the raw edges of the design. Pin in place.

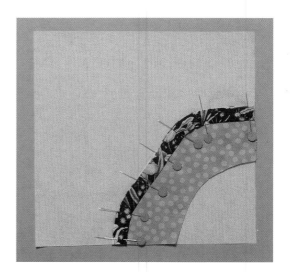

3. Stitch through the layers, ¼" away from the raw edges.

4. Finger-press the bias to cover the raw edges. Trim the underneath raw edges if they extend beyond the finger-pressed bias edging.

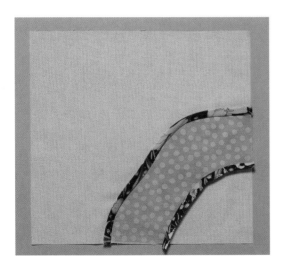

5. Construct the quilt as usual. If the bias edging runs to the edge of the block, make sure the edging is finger-pressed in the correct position before sewing the blocks together.

6. Layer and quilt. Secure the loose bias edging as you quilt. You can also stitch near the edge with a straight stitch or use fun decorative stitching.

When it comes to the sewing stages, don't forget one of the best adages: If you fail to prepare, be prepared to fail. Occasionally, great quilts probably do just happen, but I imagine this to be less often than one would like to think. Preparation is the key word behind most great quilts. I urge you to review the chapter on Hints, Tips & Useful Information beginning on page 8 before embarking on any of the quilts in Part II, as well as read the sections that follow. Starching the fabrics at the outset is every bit as important to these new methods as it was for the Really Sharp Piecing techniques, maybe even more so. Therefore, before you commence with any project, read the pattern thoroughly to get a clear understanding, and starch your fabrics well, not forgetting the ones you plan to use for the bias bindings.

In Defense of Bias

For some reason, the term *bias binding* is one that has long been maligned by being directly linked to the word "difficult." I'm not saying that people consider it difficult to use bias binding; it's making this binding that seems to cause the anguish. I don't think this is because people consider it even particularly difficult to do; just troublesome. Also, I found the method of making it with sewn "tubes" to be confusing, not just once but every time I used it. Forget all about making those fabric tubes from which you cut "continuous bias binding" because in my opinion, therein lies the culprit. What's so special about bias binding that it has to come off the fabric continuously? And isn't the straight binding on a quilt continuous? In the following sections you will find some of the ways I deal with bindings, bias or otherwise.

How Much Fabric?

Maybe this is where all the mystery surrounding bias binding starts. It shouldn't, because there is a very simple formula for figuring out what size square of fabric you will require to yield a given amount of bias binding. It is mathematical so just make friends with a calculator. First, establish the length of binding you require and then multiply that by the width you intend to cut the strips. Finally, push the square root button on your calculator to reveal the size square you need.

As an example, let's say we need 320" of bias binding. The binding is going to be cut 1¼" wide. Multiply 320 by 1.25 to give 400. Push the square root button on the calculator and it will then say 20. I would add a couple of inches onto this just for comfort and therefore use a 22" square.

Cutting the Bias Binding

Just cut your strips as you would for any other straight binding; the only difference being that you will have your fabric lying on the cutting board in a different position.

1. **Place the square of fabric diagonally on the cutting board. Lift the bottom corner and fold the fabric in half to form a triangle. The starch will help you finger-press the fold flat.**
2. **Lay your rotary ruler in the center of the triangle, placing one of the lines of the ruler on the fold to give a straight cut.**

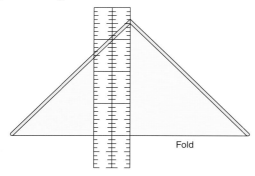

Place the square diagonally, fold in half, and lay ruler in center.

3. **Cut through the entire width. From now on, handle with care. Gently flip the triangle and place it exactly on top of the other triangle. Make sure you have the folded edges even. If you feel at all unsure about this, cut one triangle at a time.**
4. **Cut strips the same way you would if you were cutting a normal width of fabric; you'll be cutting from a triangle instead of a rectangle.**

As you work your way across the triangles, you may need to re-straighten the cutting edges as you would if cutting ordinary strips. Try to move the triangles around as little as possible during the cutting process and you won't have to straighten the edges as often. I find I can quite happily use even the short strips cut from the corner of the triangles.

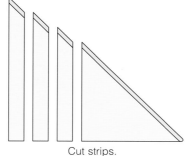

Cut strips.

Joining Strips to Make Binding

Joining strips is another area that causes undue concern. When joining the strips, whether for straight or bias binding, it is a very good idea to join the strips with angled seams rather than straight ones. This will distribute the bulk of the seams more evenly. I have a feeling that the concerns with joining stem from trying to join in a perfect 1/4" seam allowance AND with perfectly even edges along the join. This is all very well and fine and my many workmanship awards are testimony to the fact that I do care about my seams but I wish I could get students to worry just a little less about the seam allowance when joining the strips. There are basically two types of joins.

Joining Strips with Angled Ends

Usually the bias strips will have an angled end. You do not need to take the time to trim these into a true 45° angled cut. I always find it a little confusing when it comes to sewing these strips together and if I just sew without first checking, I have often ended up with a rather useless piece of V-shaped binding. When that occurs, cut off the seam and start over. To prevent this, lay the pieces down, right side up, and place them so the raw edges fit together to form one long line.

Lay pieces so raw edges fit together.

1. **Take the piece on the right and flip it over so the pieces are right sides together. Sew across the ends, inserting the machine needle into the V-shape angle to start the line and completing the sewing by aiming for the V-shape at the end. Do not get hung up about your 1/4" seam allowance. It doesn't make the least bit of difference; the important thing is starting and finishing through the "V." Chain-piece one piece after the other but do check that you are not twisting the pieces as you join.**

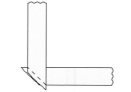

Place right sides together and stitch.

2. Cut the threads between each seam and trim the dog ears that extend beyond the seam. This will make a much neater finish.

3. Finger-press the seam allowances open and fold the binding in half, wrong sides together, with the long edges even. Press, keeping the raw edges even so that the binding will remain a constant width.

Joining Strips with Straight-Cut Ends

If you are using strips of binding with straight-cut ends, there is a very simple way to effectively join them.

1. **Lay one strip right side up and place the other on top of it with right sides together at 90°. Make sure the short ends overlap.**

That way you don't have to bother to trim the ends to a true 90°. This also makes the sewing easier since you sew the seam the same way the angled strips above were joined. This will give a perfect join every time.

2. **Trim the seam allowance and press as described above.**

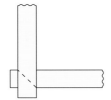

Place right sides together and stitch.

When joining binding of a predetermined measurement there will not be any overlap available beyond the ends, but you still just sew a diagonal seam corner to corner.

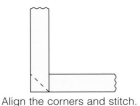

Align the corners and stitch.

Sewing the Binding Onto Curved Shapes

This is as straightforward as any line of sewing and there are only a couple of points to remember. First, if at all possible, be sure to use a sewing machine foot that has been specifically designed for sewing the quilter's ¼"

seam. This should really apply to all ¼" seams. There is one of these feet available to fit almost all makes and models of machines these days. Please take the time to make sure that when using this foot you are correctly positioning the fabric in relation to the foot to actually produce the intended ¼" seam. This really is a case of once sorted, always sorted and truly worth doing.

If you hold the fabrics to be sewn slightly to the left in front of the needle, they will feed under the machine smoothly, giving a more dependable ¼" seam allowance. Remember, when sewing on any binding, the uniformity of the finished binding width is determined by sewing a consistent seam allowance throughout.

Joining Binding on Quilt Edges

I have included this not because I wish to enter into general quiltmaking techniques but because this is an area that I used to struggle with. I want my final join for the binding ends to be the same as all the others throughout the quilt.

1. **Stitch the binding onto the edge of the quilt, beginning about 6" from one side of a corner and leaving a loose tail of binding about 6" long. Sew the binding to the quilt in the normal way, using the folding method to create miters at each corner. Stop stitching when you get to within 6" of the starting point.**

2. **Lay the quilt edge flat and smooth the loose ends of binding into the position where they should be sewn down, making them meet in the center of the unstitched gap. Fold the strips back where they meet and finger-press along the fold.**

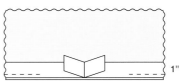

Fold strips and finger-press.

3. **Measure and trim each 2"-wide strip 1¼" away from the fold. Pin the edges of the quilt together so the ends are left free and the weight of the quilt is not pulling on the binding ends.**

4. **Fold the quilt in half and pin through the spot where the stitching started and stopped. Open**

both strips out and place the ends at a 90° angle to each other, right sides together. Join the strips with a diagonal seam as shown below.

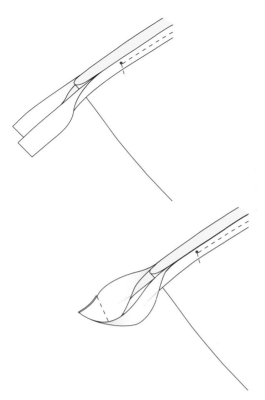

Open strips, place ends at a 90°-angle, and stitch.

5. Trim the seam to ¼" and press it open.

This method is fairly foolproof and I never cease to feel a thrill of secret surprise as I lay the quilt edge out flat and watch the binding pop into position, giving no more and no less than an exact fit. Now that's what I call cooperative binding!

Non-Stop Circles

When sewing bias binding onto a circle it is easier to join the ends of the binding before sewing it onto the circle. This works best with circles 15" or less in diameter, but if you pin well, you can also use this method with larger circles.

The next question is how to determine the length of binding to use to get the circle to fit properly. I have consulted at great length with my numerically gifted husband and have gleaned several useful bits of information. He managed to clear up a few things that have remained a mystery to me ever since I stopped listening in geometry class many years ago.

For a start, I now know in the simplest of terms how to find the circumference of a circle. This is all I really need to allow me to know how long to cut my binding. Peter loves tossing in words like "pi" when telling me all this but little does he know, I don't even listen. According to him, pi (and he would much prefer I use the proper symbol π) equals 22 divided by 7. Determining the circumference of a circle is as easy as this: π multiplied by the diameter of the circle equals the circumference.

I personally have no interest in pi unless it's spelled with an *E* at the end. I worry that after the last few sentences those of you who share my mathematical tendencies will be tempted to opt out. Never fear! It is truly easy to find the distance around the outside of a circle and thus how long the binding needs to be cut. The best way to convey this is by giving an example:

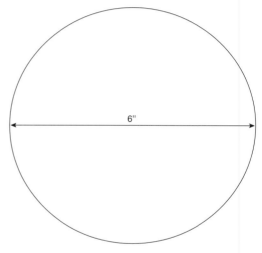

$$22 \div 7 = 3.1428571; \ 3.1428571 \times 6" = 18.857142$$

The chart on page 79 shows that .857142 would be rounded to ⅞". So, the circumference of a 6" circle would be 18⅞" for the purposes of patchwork. Quite frankly, I find 18⅞" to be far less intimidating than 18.857142. If you happen to be in the minority who actually understands and enjoys working with numbers, please forgive what appears to be a rather patronizing assumption that I feel no quilters are mathematically inclined. Not so, but I think all would agree that the majority are not.

Decimal Equivalents for Inches

.125 =	1/8
.25 =	1/4
.375 =	3/8
.5 =	1/2
.625 =	5/8
.75 =	3/4
.875 =	7/8

When cutting the binding for a 6" circle, cut a length of bias binding 19⅜" long. This is the circumference of the circle plus ½" for the seam allowances. The ends should be square and not angle cut. Then, sew the ends together as discussed on page 76, using a diagonal seam, with the strips placed right sides together, ends at 90°.

The folded bias binding can be sewn on with one circular line of stitching and no obvious joins.

Ideally, I would like to be able to give you a formula for joining the strips with an angled seam from a measured amount of binding. My resident mathematical consultant assures me that it is possible but we have not resolved this yet, which only leaves me to say, "Watch this space" and "Any theories welcomed" because it really would be a very helpful formula to know.

Free-Form Shapes

The above method works very well for circles but what about free-form, hand-drawn shapes, which are so useful in modern designs. My solution is rather unsophisticated but it works. I simply take a non-stretch piece of twine, tape one end of it onto the drawn line, and then carefully lay the string on the line until it meets the taped end of string. Mark and then measure the string by laying it flat on your cutting board. I always repeat this whole procedure several times to check for accuracy. Add ½" seam allowance to the measurement, then cut and sew the binding in the same way as described to the left for circles. Upon reading this, Peter's comment was "Humph!" but I notice he didn't offer any alternative to my less-than-scientific method, which means that he actually agrees with me if truth be known.

Quilting Down the Binding

Quilt down the binding at the same time as doing any other machine quilting. When the binding is stitched down simultaneously with the quilting stitches, it is not only a real timesaver but I feel the boost of being super-efficient for a change. The threads can be whatever you choose, using any stitch you prefer from straight to fancy. Use your fingers to press the binding into position as you come to them. By and large, I feel that this sort of work is best done machine-guided rather than with free-motion quilting. If you should find an area where the seam allowance seems as though it will protrude from under the sewn binding, trim the seam allowance before quilting down the binding.

Gone Fishin'

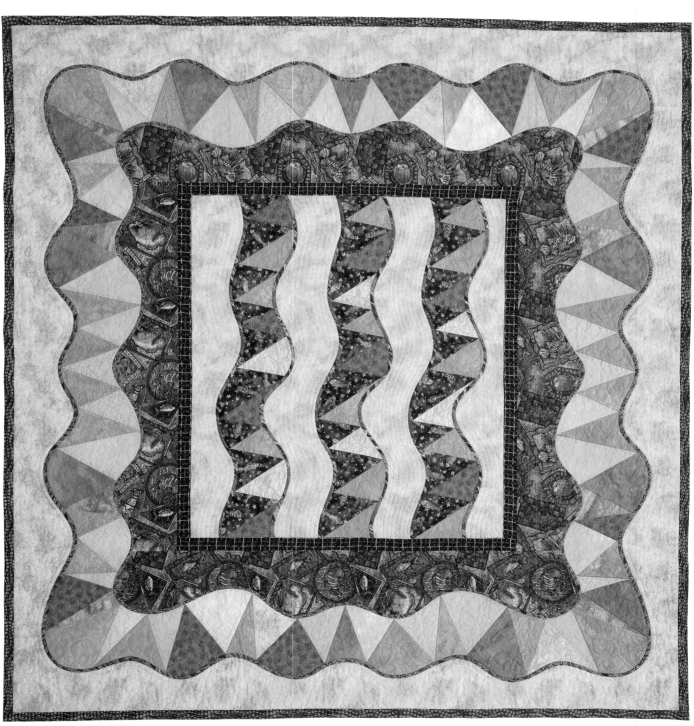

Gone Fishin', 75'' x 79½'', designed by Barbara Barber, developed and constructed by Linda Park, Westborough, Massachusetts

In *Gone Fishin'*, foundation piecing is combined with bias binding, with a great deal of design freedom thrown in. This was a very exciting quilt to design because it barely touches the tip of the iceberg when it comes to innovative new possibilities put within easy reach of all quilters, whatever their skill levels and abilities. I gave Linda Park a drawing and the main fabrics. She took them, enhanced them with ideas and fabrics of her own, and came up with a result I absolutely love. It is seeing the reality of a vision I had a good while back.

Materials

- **Yellow #1:** 1⅛ yards yellow fabric for center panel
- **Dark Blue Fish Print:** 1 yard for foundation strips in center panel
- **Light Blues:** 1 yard total for foundation strips in center panel
- **Stripe:** ⅔ yard for bias binding in center panel
- **Dark Print:** ⅓ yard for narrow inner border around center panel
- **Large Fish Print:** 1⅔ yards for middle border
- **Yellow #2:** 2¼ yards for outer border
- **Various Yellows:** 10 fat quarters for foundation strips in outer border
- **Various Blues:** 11 fat quarters for foundation strips in outer border
- **Contrasting Print:** ⅞ yard for bias binding in outer border
- **Blue Print:** 2 yards for edge binding
- 4¾ yards backing
- 79" x 84" batting
- Freezer paper (optional)

Photocopies/Tracing

NOTE: The patterns on the pullout are reduced. They need to be enlarged 200%.

- 3 copies or tracings of the complete center panel strip
- 2 copies of complete side border strips
- 2 copies of complete top and bottom border strips

Cutting

Yellow #1
- Cut 1 rectangle 34½" x 39" for center panel.

Dark Blue Fish Print
- Cut as you foundation piece the foundation strips in center panel.

Light Blues
- Cut as you foundation piece the foundation strips in center panel.

Stripe
- Cut 1¼"-wide bias strips from a 20" x 20" square. Prepare as described in the chapter on New Ideas and New Techniques to make approximately 270" of bias binding for center panel.

Dark Print
- Cut 2 strips 2" x 39" and 2 strips 2" x 37½" for narrow inner border around center panel.

Large Fish Print
- Cut 2 lengthwise strips 10" x 42" and 2 lengthwise strips 10" x 56½" for the middle border.

Yellow #2
- Cut 2 lengthwise strips 9¾" x 61½" and 2 lengthwise strips 9¾" x 75" for the outer border.

Various Yellows
- Cut as you foundation piece the foundation strips in outer border.

Various Blues
- Cut as you foundation piece the foundation strips in outer border.

Contrasting Print
- Cut 1¼"-wide bias strips from a 27" square. Prepare as described in the chapter on New Ideas and New Techniques to make approximately 530" of bias binding for the outer pieced borders.

Foundation-Pieced Unit Construction

Sewing the Foundation-Pieced Units

Trim the paper for the center panel and border strips so there is a ¼" seam allowance.

Because this free-form design uses pieces of varying widths, don't cut the fabrics for foundation piecing all at once, but rather as you work, gauging each piece as you come to it. In the photograph below, you can see how a large ruler can be used under the foundation to guide the cutting of these pieces. To do this, lay the fabric you wish to cut on your cutting mat and place a rotary ruler on top of a corner section that is roughly the required size—you will get better and better at judging this. Position the foundation pattern over the ruler so that there is sufficient ruler and fabric under the pattern to comfortably cover the section of the pattern you are working with. Cutting the piece with room to spare may use more fabric, but it will save you headaches! Refer to Size of Pieces, page 11, for more information.

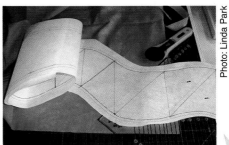

Photo: Linda Park

NOTE: Linda made two identical outer border units for the sides and two identical units for the top/bottom with regard to color and fabric placement. When inverted and put into position this is not immediately noticeable but it probably helped with the overall sense of balance. Each section of pieced outer border starts and stops with the same blue fabric.

1. Use the dark blue fish print and the light blue fabrics to foundation piece the 3 foundation strips for the center panel, reviewing the section on Straight-Unit Piecing on page 39 if necessary. Trim the strips to include the 1/4" seam allowance.

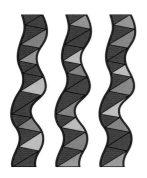

2. Use the various yellow and blue fabrics to foundation piece the 4 foundation strips for the outer border. Trim the strips to include the 1/4" seam allowance.

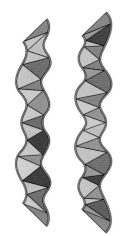

Side top/bottom, make 2 of each.

3. Carefully remove the paper from the 3 foundation strips for the center panel. To do this, lay the units, paper side up, flat on the tabletop to remove the pattern without distortion. Do not remove the paper until you are ready to attach it to the background because with excessive handling it could stretch, although a good starching at the outset will help prevent such problems.

Attaching the Foundation Strips to the Center Panel

1. It may appear complex but *Gone Fishin'* requires very little accuracy and this is reflected in the method used to establish the positions for the 3 foundation strips on the central panel. The easiest method is to fold the yellow center panel into four equal sections and crease it along the three folds. The spray starch should make it possible to do this with finger pressing but if not, use your iron.

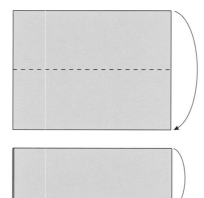

2. Place the yellow panel flat on a work space and lay each of the three pieced units over one of the creased folds, centering them by eye and using straight pins to hold them in place until the stitching is completed.

3. Sew the bias binding and the foundation units onto the background with one line of stitching down each side of the piecing.

4. Press the edges of the binding away from the pieced "appliqués." The edge of the binding remains loose at this time.

Adding the Borders

1. Stitch the 2" x 39" narrow inner border strips to both side edges of the center panel. Press the seam allowances for all straight border sections toward the edges of the quilt.

2. Sew the 2" x 37½" border strips to the top and bottom of the center panel. Press.

3. Add the 10" x 42" fish print middle borders to the sides and the 10" x 56½" fish print middle borders to the top and bottom. Press.

4. Sew the 9¾" x 61½" yellow outer border strips to both sides and the 9¾" x 75" yellow outer borders strips to the top and bottom. Press.

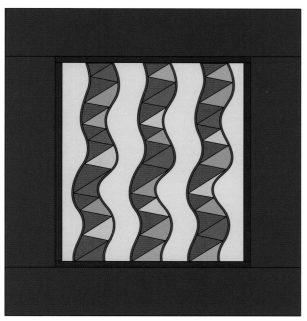

Add middle border.

Add outer border.

Appliquéing the Pieced Border

1. Join the corners of the pieced "frame" before removing the paper pattern. With right sides together, pin and then stitch, using the straight line at the ends of each pattern as a stitching line. Press the seams open.

2. At this stage, you should have what looks like a big fabric picture frame. Carefully remove the paper foundation. The seam connecting the fish border to the yellow border will lie underneath the wavy pieced "appliqué." This seam makes a very good guide for placement of the "appliqué." Place the pieced frame over the seam, centering it by eye and holding in place with pins. Refer to page 77, Sewing the Binding Onto Curved Shapes. As before, stitch the bias binding and the foundation frame permanently into position.

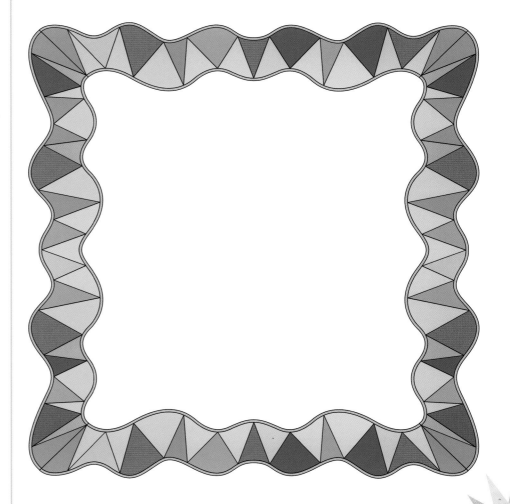

Finishing

1. Layer and baste.

2. Stitch all the loose edges of the bias bindings in place as you quilt. Use whatever type of quilting you fancy. The quilting was not marked on the quilt top; it was done in a free-form manner.

3. *Gone Fishin'* has a wide outer edge binding that contributes quite a bit to the overall effect. Cut 6"-wide bias strips from 2 squares 33" x 33" for 320" of double-fold binding.

Sew the binding onto the quilt using a 1" seam allowance and stopping the stitching 1" in from the edge at each corner instead of the normal 1/4" to form a fold miter. To get a miter when stitching on wider-than-normal bindings your seam allowances must be the same width as you want the finished binding to be and you must stop sewing that same amount in from the edge of the quilt at each corner.

These days, most quilters know how to form a miter on the bindings of their quilts. If you have any questions, look up bindings in any basic quiltmaking book and you will find detailed instructions. *All About Quilting from A to Z* (C&T Publishing) is an excellent and up-to-date reference book with clear photography and illustrations throughout, suitable for quilters of all skill levels.

What Ifs

Look for new ways and designs in which to develop the techniques. In the quilt *Leap Frog*, page 68, you can see how easy it is to make a complex-looking quilt simply by making units and tacking them down on a square of fabric, with the machine quilting stitches finally holding the binding edges in place. In other projects, the technique is used to make straight units, curves, and circles in the same way.

Take a look at the image below and compare it with the photograph of the completed *Gone Fishin'* quilt, page 80. Here you can see what it would look like without any of the foundation-pieced, binding-edged units; just the constructional seams. It does, in fact, look pretty boring and probably not a quilt anyone would want to make. It certainly does not look as interesting as the completed *Gone Fishin'*.

Making it could not be simpler and you can see that for yourself by combining the units below with the previous image to make the final design. All you have to do is mentally lay these pieces over the first photograph and you have summed up what the actual making of this quilt amounts to. Really, it is simple and that's saying something when you think of a complicated-looking design like *Gone Fishin'*.

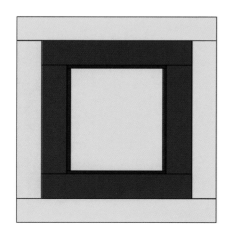 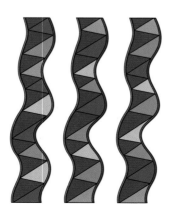 

The three foundation-pieced units are sewn onto the yellow background at the same time as the bias binding. This is done before the borders are sewn around the center in order to catch the binding within that seam. In the outer border, the foundation-pieced frame is laid over the seam that joins the yellow border to the large blue fish print. Finally, after the quilt is layered and pinned for the quilting, you will appliqué and quilt the foundation-pieced units while stitching the loose edge of the binding into its permanent position. This stitching can be plain or decorative, depending on the quilt and the type of effect you wish to achieve.

If you are designing a quilt like *Gone Fishin'*, remember that it is your quilt and you can plan it to be whatever size you like, with as many borders as you fancy, or for that matter, without any borders at all. The foundation-pieced units can have straight sides instead of the wavy edges. These units can be completely free-form, drawn by hand, to give a truly wonky effect. Before you commit yourself to anything, stop to consider just a few of the endless possibilities. These are all good, fun reasons to design your own. So often, I hear students say, "I have to follow a pattern. I could never come up with my own design." That simply is not true. Yes, you do have to be willing to ask "What if?" and "What about trying?" but there's nothing to be lost with such speculation and it's actually a great deal of fun. Consider the following to get your mind working along these lines.

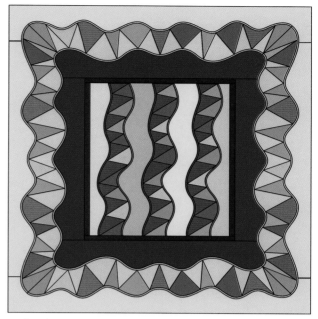

Sew four vertical strips of four different colors and prints together to make up a center panel and then appliqué the foundation-pieced units on top of the seamlines.

Sew horizontal strips together to make the center panel and then appliqué foundation-pieced units to cover the seams.

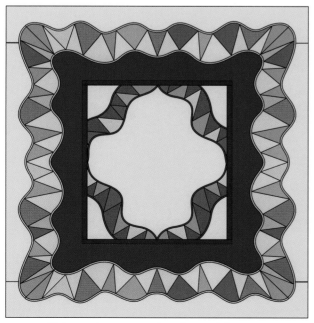

Cut a center square, place it on point, sew on corners, and attach foundation-pieced units diagonally over those seams.

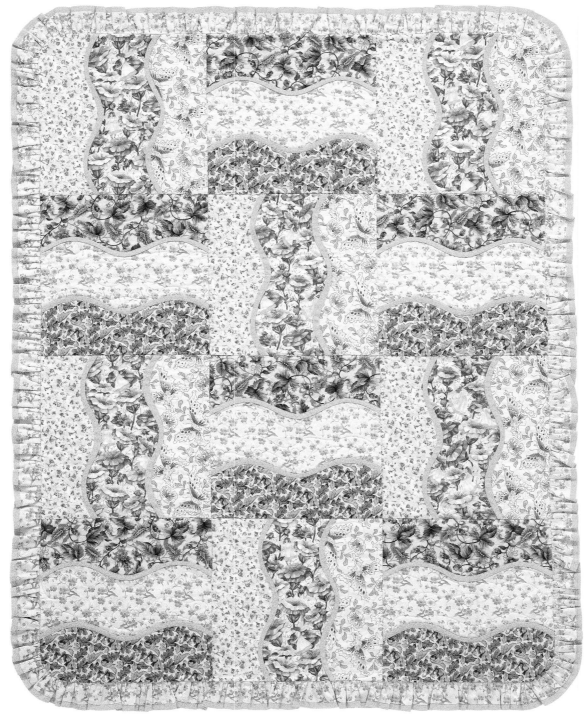

Nana's Ruffles, 43" x 56", Linda Park, Westborough, Massachusetts

I gave Linda a rough drawing with instructions that what I wanted to illustrate was how a very simple design could be very effective. It was to be a really quick quilt made without the foundation-pieced sections but using the general ideas from *Gone Fishin'*. When I saw the finished quilt I gasped with delight and pure pleasure at the simple beauty of the timeless color scheme and design. When I commented on how much I love the yellow and blue together Linda said a beautiful thing, "Everyone does, but those colors belong to Nana; she's just very kindly lent them to the rest of us." Sadly, Linda lost her beloved Nana, at the graceful age of 105, shortly after this.

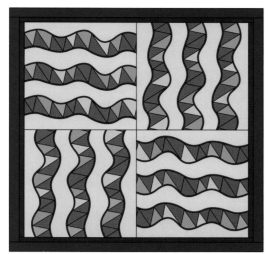

Make four square panels, rotate them,
and sew them together.

Again, the choice is yours; straight or wavy edges to the outside of your quilt.

Whether or not you actually choose to make any of your design ideas into real quilts is not important. You will have strengthened your design muscles and as with most things, it's a case of "use it or lose it."

Read through the pattern for *Gone Fishin'* even if you don't intend to make this particular quilt. You will see how the pattern was made so, if you choose, you can make your own pattern for your own unique design. It is astoundingly easier than the photograph of the quilt would lead you to believe.

Lay a foundation-pieced frame around
the edge of the quilt.

Lay the foundation-pieced frame over a
wider border section, finishing the quilt
with a straight edge.

Leave off the final border and end
with a wavy edge.

Sew multiple borders of varying sizes around a central square and then lay foundation-pieced frames over the
seamlines. This would be ring-pieced but the rings would be appliquéd with bias binding along the edges.

Leap Frog

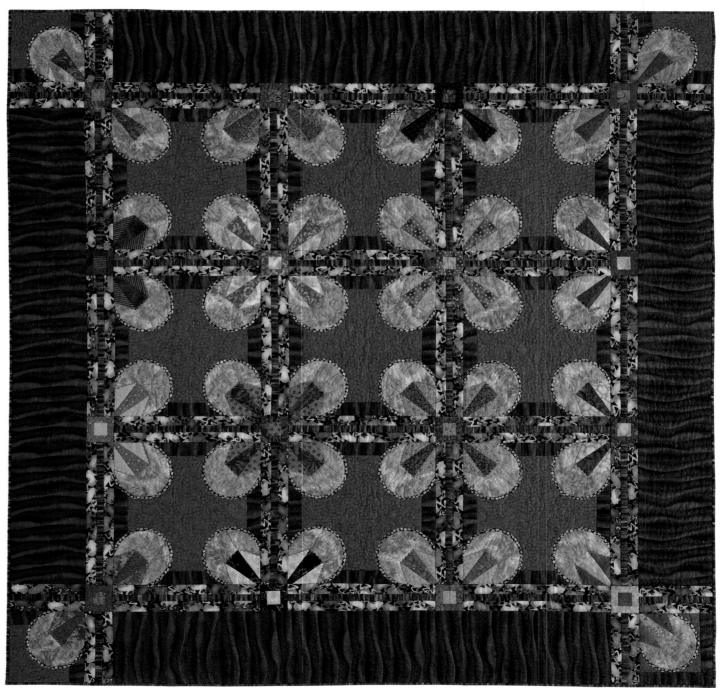

Leap Frog, 76½" x 76½", Barbara Barber, Hampshire, England

I used the bias binding techniques in blocks rather than with long strips of piecing in this quilt. The possibilities are as limitless as the shapes one can dream up.

Materials

- **Bright Blue Texture:** 1½ yards for background of blocks and corner squares in border
- **Green Stripe:** 1⅓ yards for middle strip of pieced sashing and edge binding
- **Lime Green Texture:** 2 yards for lily pads
- **Frog Print:** 1⅓ yards for sashing strips
- **Pink/Blue Stripe:** 2½ yards for borders and blocks
- **Assorted Pinks:** 2 yards total for A, B, and setting blocks in sashing
- **Green Print:** 1 yard for bias binding on lily pads
- 4½ yards for backing
- 80" x 80" batting

Photocopies

- 40 photocopies of the *Leap Frog* Flower pattern, pages 92–93

NOTE: You can fit 4 of these on a standard-size sheet of paper.

Cutting

Bright Blue Texture

- Cut 9 squares 13½" x 13½" for the background of the blocks.
- Cut 4 squares 7" x 7" for the corner squares in the border.

Green Stripe

NOTE: The stripe in the cut pieces will run across the narrower measurement.

- Cut 12 crosswise strips 1¼" wide. From these strips cut 24 strips 1¼" x 16½" for center strip in sashing.
- Cut 2 crosswise strips 1¼" wide. From these strips cut 8 strips 1¼" x 8½" for the sashing that continues into the border.

Lime Green Texture

- Cut 40 pieces using Lily Pad pattern, page 93. See Photocopied Templates, page 27, for suggested methods.

Frog Print

- Cut 24 strips 1⅝" wide. From these strips, cut 48 strips 1⅝" x 16½" for the outer strips in the sashing.
- Cut 4 strips 1⅝" wide. From these strips, cut 16 strips 1⅝" x 8½" for the sashing that continues into the border.

Pink/Blue Stripe

NOTE: The stripe in the cut pieces will run across the narrower measurement.

- Cut 6 crosswise strips 8½" wide. Sew these strips together end to end and cut into 4 strips 54½" long for the borders.
- Cut 6 crosswise strips 2" wide. From these strips cut 18 strips 2" x 13½" for the blocks.
- Cut 9 crosswise strips 2" wide. From these strips cut 18 strips 2" x 16½" for the blocks.
- Cut 2 crosswise strips 2" wide. From these strips cut 4 strips 2" x 8½" and 4 strips 2" x 7" for the corner blocks.

Assorted Pinks

- Cut 40 pieces using the Flower Pattern A, page 92. They do not need to be accurately cut since they will be foundation pieced.
- Cut 80 pieces each 2¼" x 5½" for the B's: they will be foundation pieced and this is a minimum measurement for cutting but there is no need for accuracy.
- Cut 16 squares 2" x 2" for the centers of the setting squares in the sashing.
- Cut 32 strips 1¼" x 2" for the top and bottom of the setting squares in the sashing.
- Cut 32 strips 1¼" x 3½" for the sides of the setting squares in the sashing.

Green Print

- Cut 1¼"-wide bias strips from a square 32" x 32" for 720" for bias edging on lily pads, following the instructions in New Ideas and New Techniques, page 74.

Foundation-Pieced Flowers

1. Cut out the photocopies of the *Leap Frog* flower pattern, page 92. These paper patterns need to be cut out with scissors, exactly on

the solid line on the top three sides and along the broken or dashed lines for the bottom two edges.

2. Place a piece of fabric cut for the Flower Template A wrong side up on the table and center the paper pattern over the top. Balance the excess fabric around the outside of the lines of the A piece on the pattern and insert a straight pin to hold in position.

Center pattern on fabric and pin.

3. Lay one of the 2¼" x 5½" pink rectangles on the work surface, right side up. Position the paper pattern over the top as shown and pin in place.

Position pinned unit on top of the rectangle and pin.

4. Set your sewing machine to a short stitch for paper piecing. Start stitching from the 90° corner, beginning just off the edge of the paper. Stitch on the line through to the other edge but do not stitch off the edge of the paper. Backstitch for about ¼" to secure the ends and remove from

machine. Finger-press open. Sew the other side of the flower unit. Press.

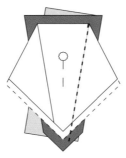

Stitch from 90° corner.

5. Turn the flower unit over so that the paper is on top and place it on an ironing surface. Bring the seam allowance that protrudes above the top of the flower unit down over the paper, gently pulling it against the paper template. Press this well to form a good crease.

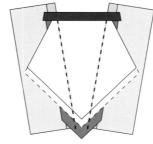

Turn unit over, bring the center seam allowance over the paper, and press.

6. The following may seem a bit tricky when you read it but it is far more straightforward when you're actually doing it. Trim the extra fabric from the side rectangles ¼" away from the solid lines. Press the seam allowances for each side of the flower down over the paper template in a similar fashion. Press the little fabric dog-ear of seam allowance down in the way you find gives the neatest, sharpest angle. Don't get bogged down with worry about this because if you try it several

different ways you'll find it's rather like wrapping an awkward parcel; after you've wrapped one or two it looks like you're a professional. DO NOT remove the paper patterns just yet.

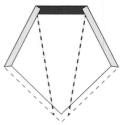

Bring the side seam allowances over the paper, and press.

Block Construction

1. Sew the pink/blue pieces to the sides of the blue background squares: add the shorter ones first to opposite sides of the 13½" squares. Press the seams toward the outsides.

2. Sew the two longer strips onto the squares. Press.

Attach the strips.

3. Position the green lily pads on top of the pieced background square. Align the 90° corners to give true corners and pin. Lay the raw edges of the prepared bias binding even with the curved edge of the lily pad and begin stitching. The ends of the bias should extend beyond the edges of the block to assure coverage once the bias is

pressed open. Finger-press the binding over the seam allowances.

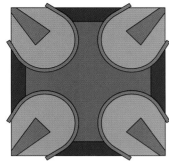

Align the 90° corners and add the bias binding to the curved edge.

4. Carefully remove the paper patterns from the flower units one by one just before you pin them in position on top of the lily pads in the corner of the block. Pin well to prevent shifting during sewing. You may, in fact, find it easier to prevent movement by sewing with a walking foot. Sew near the edge of the flower unit using a contrasting thread and the very largest machine stitch your sewing machine will offer you. This will be used solely as a basting stitch and you will have to remove it later.

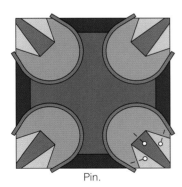

Pin.

Sashing Construction

1. Sew a $1^5/8$" x $16^1/2$" frog print strip to each side of the $1^1/4$" x $16^1/2$" green stripe pieces to make the sashing units. You will need 24.

2. Construct the setting squares for the sashing in exactly the same

way as you prepared the background for the main blocks. You will need to make 16 of these $3^1/2$" squares.

Quilt Top Construction

1. Following the layout for the quilt, sew the center together. To do this, sew the units into rows and then sew the rows together. Press the block rows toward the sashing and the sashing rows toward the setting squares.

2. Make 4 corner blocks. These are made in exactly the same way as the main blocks but are a quarter version of that larger block.

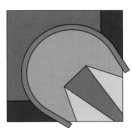

Corner Block

Quilt Construction

3. Sew 8 sashing units for the border in the same way as the longer sashing units were prepared for the center.

4. Attach one of these sashing units to each end of the $54^1/2$" x $8^1/2$" pink/blue stripe border pieces. Sew 2 of these border units to opposite sides of the quilt center. Press toward the border.

5. Attach a corner block to each end of the two remaining long border units. Sew these to the top and bottom of the quilt center. Press toward the border.

Finishing

1. Layer and baste the quilt.

2. Quilt as desired to finish your quilt. Be sure to quilt all of the bindings down and permanently stitch the flower units in position. Remove the basting stitches before starting to sew each flower. It is easier to remove the basting before stitching over the previous row of stitches. The flowers will not unfold at this stage because the basting stitches have given them a nice strong crease. You may find it a nice idea to use a fancy stitch or thread to do this.

3. Bind the quilt with 2"-wide bias strips cut from a 27" green stripe square.

An Observation

As quilters, we often like to think that we are of an observant nature. Or at least I used to like to think I was—*Leap Frog* proved me wrong. I guess what it boils down to is some people are and some people aren't. Are you? Have you spotted what is wrong with my quilt *Leap Frog*? Yes, alright, this is just an elaborate ploy to cover up an error in one of the corner blocks that I didn't notice until the quilt was completely finished. Needless to say, I decided it "added to the charm," or as others would say, it was my "deliberate mistake."

Leap Frog Flower Pattern

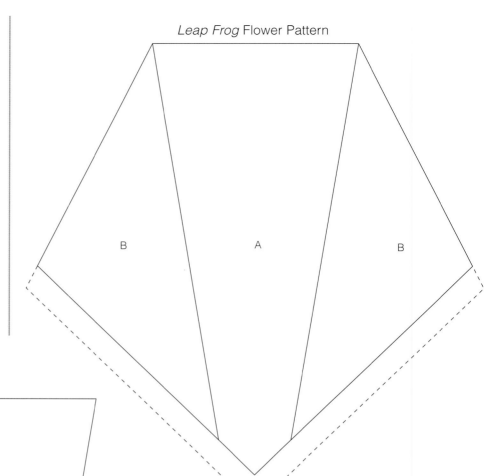

B A B

Flower Pattern

A

Detail of *Across the Pond,* Janet Benjafield, Devon, England

Lily Pad Pattern

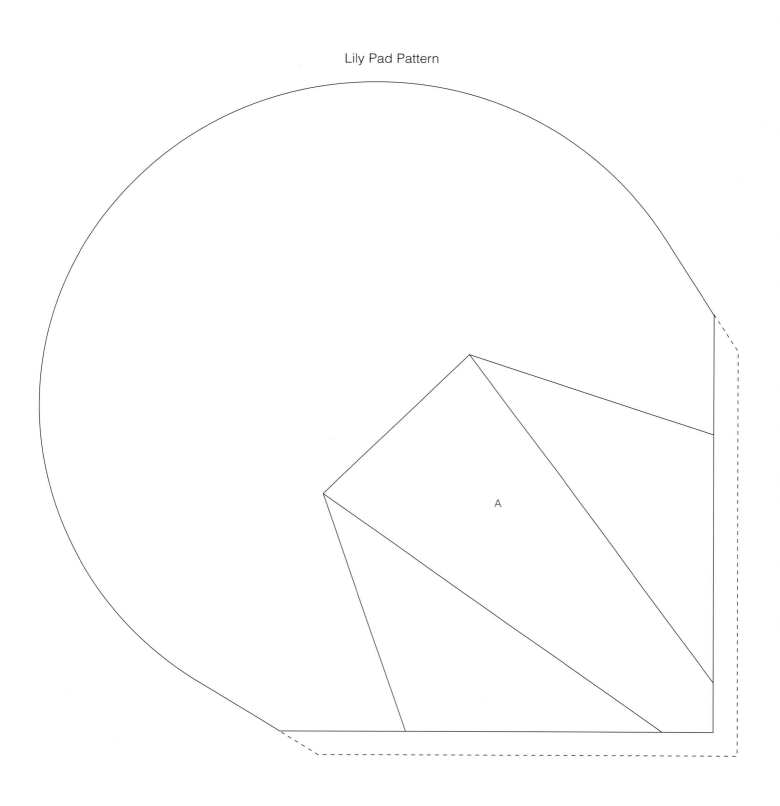

A

I urge you to take a look through the blocks shown here to get your creative juices flowing. I'm sure that for the most part, curved shapes work best and are the most straightforward as far as making goes, but *Irish Stars* illustrates that the bias can be used on angled shapes as well.

Also, be sure to look at the three variations of *Leap Frog* that students have made. These are shown in the

Gallery, beginning on page 61, and I have to say, in all honesty, I prefer each of theirs to my own. My inspiration was simple in that I had a frog fabric and a blue fabric that were begging to be used. The general idea was one of lily pads and flowers, but if you're not keen on that don't worry because I don't feel that *Wild Thing*, page 71, misses the frogs in the least little bit!

Irish Stars, 74" x 74", Barbara Barber, Hampshire, England. Collection of Mary Holloway, Hampshire, England

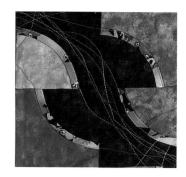

Dots Gone Crazy

Dots Gone Crazy, 63½'' x 63½'', Barbara Barber, Hampshire, England

It was a natural progression to make the jump from the curved shapes of *Leap Frog* to going full-circle. Even though it was natural curiosity that started me playing with circles and bias binding in the first place, the true incentive was to come up with a technique for making one of my all time favorite patterns, Drunkard's Path. In all of my workshops, I have never seen so great a quantity of quality work, produced in such a short time, by such a happy lot.

Materials

- **Mottled Black:** 2¾ yards for blocks and border
- **Assorted Mottled Brights:** 3 yards total for blocks and border
- **Bright Print:** 1¾ yards for the bias binding on the blocks, border, and edge binding
- 3⅞ yards for backing
- 68" x 68" batting
- Creative Grid rulers (optional)

Before starting to make a block or the quilt please review New Ideas and New Techniques, page 74, and prepare your fabrics accordingly. Also, be aware that you will need 144 little blocks and that 72 will be made from one color arrangement and 72 will be made using the same colors but in the opposite way.

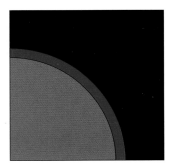

Block color arrangement; make 72.

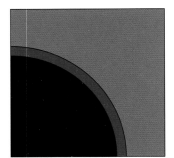

Block color arrangement; make 72.

Don't despair when you read that 144 blocks are required. One of the great things about this method is that you will make 4 at a time and that's only 36 sets; 18 sets of each color arrangement.

Cutting

NOTE: The 9½" and 7" squares do not have to be cut accurately since they will be trimmed to size later.

Mottled Black
NOTE: Cut the lengthwise border strips first.

- Cut 8 lengthwise strips 2½" x 56" for the border.
- From the remaining 22" width of fabric, cut 5 crosswise strips 9½" wide. From the remaining 42" width of fabric, cut 2 crosswise strips 9½" wide. From these strips, cut 18 squares 9½" x 9½" for blocks.

Assorted Mottled Brights
- Cut 18 squares 7" x 7" for blocks.
- Cut strips that vary in width from 2" to 4" wide.

Bright Print
- Cut 1 square 36" x 36". Cut into strips 1¼" wide for the bias binding on the blocks and border.

Block Construction

1. Use a ruler to draw 2 lines through the centers of the 7" squares; the lines must intersect at 90° in the center of the squares. You can guess-timate the center by eye but do make sure that the lines cross in a true perpendicular way; this will be made easier by using a clear rotary cutting ruler.

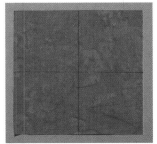

Draw 2 lines that intersect in the center.

2. Use a 6½" circle rotary ruler to cut a circle from each 7" square. I developed this technique with the Creative Grid set of circular rulers in mind and know that they have a very convenient cross through them indicating the center lines. These rules make it so easy because they also have the extra half-inch for seam allowance. If you are not using Creative Grid rulers, you will have to make your adjustments accordingly. If you use a rotary cutter with the smallest size blade for cutting circles you will find it easier and in fact, be able to cut multiple layers of four to six at a time. Be sure to line up the center cross of the ruler with the lines you drew on the squares before cutting.

3. Place a fabric circle on each of the 9½" squares, positioning by eye and making certain that the center cross remains upright. Pin.

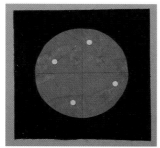

Place circles on squares and pin.

4. Make bias binding following the instructions on page 75 to provide a total length of about 975". Don't think about it, just join the strips and press the binding in half lengthwise. The number of inches just sounds bad and does, in fact, include 225" of bias binding that is used as an edging between the blocks and the border of the quilt.

5. Sew the binding around the circles, keeping the edge of the binding even with the edge of the circles. Start and end the binding at one of the quarter marks drawn onto the circle. Press the binding outward using just the tip of the iron. Guide the tip of the iron along the inner curved seam to give a smooth result. It is very important to press the bias binding outward before cutting the square/circle into four since it will almost certainly distort the squares otherwise.

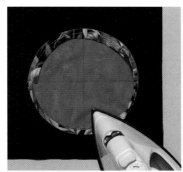

Attach binding and press.

6. Cut each square/circle in half, placing the edge of your ruler along the edge of one of the drawn lines on the circle.

Without touching or disturbing the fabric, reposition the ruler so that you are now able to cut the square/circle in half again, using a perpendicular cut.

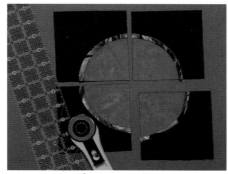

Cut into 4 units.

7. Trim the units to $4^{1}/_{2}$" x $4^{1}/_{2}$". When trimming, be aware that the corner that has the quarter-circle attached to it is already a true 90° and you should not trim it again. Place the ruler so that you can measure away from the "dotted" corner and trim the opposite sides, producing a true $4^{1}/_{2}$" unit. Make 144 units.

8. Sew 16 of the $4^{1}/_{2}$" units together to form the block (8 with black background, 8 with colored background). Make sure the loose side of the bias binding is in the correct position when sewing the blocks together. I insert pins into the binding to hold it in the finished position while sewing the block together. Make 9 blocks. Press so seams will nest.

Block Construction

Quilt Top Construction

1. Join the blocks into rows and then sew the rows together to form the center of the quilt. Press so seams will nest.

2. The brightly pieced sections can be made by foundation piecing or by just sewing random strips together at odd angles. Make 4 paper patterns that have a finished measurement of 4" x 56" and use to foundation piece these sections.

3. Leave the paper intact for the time being and add the long black strips, one to each side of the foundation-pieced sections, pressing the seam allowances toward the black.

4. Sew a strip of the remaining bias binding along one edge of the black with the raw edges even. This strip will form a flat piping and should be trimmed even with the black fabric at both ends.

Pieced-Border Construction

Add long strips.

Add strip.

5. Attach the borders to the quilt using the partial seaming technique. Start by sewing about half of one border onto the center from the left edge, leaving the other half of it unstitched for the moment.

6. Add the other borders, working your way around the quilt counter clockwise before finally going back and stitching the second half of the first border seam. Press the seam allowances toward the borders as you go.

7. Double check that the binding is in the correct position as I can assure you, this is not particularly a lesson that you wish to learn the hard way—I've already done that for you!

Finishing

1. Layer and baste the quilt.

2. My quilt was quilted in a very free-form way I used to catch the loose edges of bindings at the same time, with what was amazingly little effort. I like the effect but would say that when you start you might be slightly disappointed with the result—I was, but knew I was in too deep to stop and found that this quilting only looked good after you had added quite a few of the random quilting lines. These lines were stitched using many different colored threads to add to the multicolored effect. There are many superb variegated high-quality threads that are suitable for machine quilting and I'm sure these could give a great result, too.

3. Bind the quilt with a 2"-wide bias binding cut from a 24" x 24" square.

Quilt Construction

Stitching Detail of *Dots Gone Crazy*

Foolproof Curves

I urge you to begin looking at the possibilities using the full-circle theory. Best of all, because of the freedom this technique allows, you will be amazed at the scope of ideas that start to creep into your mind. To give you just the tiniest peek through the keyhole to this area of design, look at the *back* of Janet Benjafield's quilt, *Dots Out Back*. Janet used the methods used in Non-Stop Circles, page 78. You can see the front of her quilt in the Gallery, page 69.

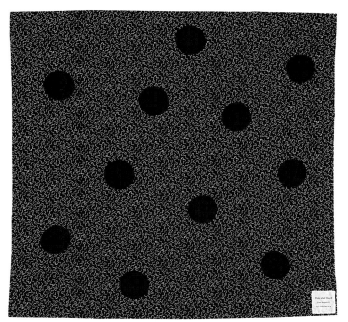

Backview of *Dots Out Back*, 72" x 72", Janet Benjafield, Devon, England

This is really fun—for you and me! Don't forget to keep a pencil and pad handy as you read this and jot down any ideas, no matter how silly you may *think* they are because they could also be *brilliant*! Again, experience has taught me that if I don't sketch the ideas as they occur, they end up simply as a fleeting thought and disappear even quicker than they came about in the first place. I can easily toss the rubbish designs into the garbage but have no hope of conjuring up thoughts lost within my head!

In the project instructions, I mentioned cutting the squares to give a perfect quarter-circle in each corner, but in this drawing of *Dots Truly Gone*, you can see what would happen if you purposely placed the circles off-center onto the background square or if these circles were not true circles in the first place.

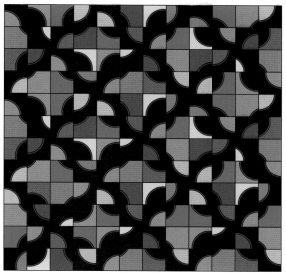

Dots Truly Gone

While doing the writing about the center for *Dots Truly Gone*, I've developed some interesting border thoughts and these use a combination of other techniques I've previously covered in this book. Take a look at this next drawing of *Dots Truly Gone* and you will see how I have used the techniques from *Leap Frog*, page 88, for the corner squares in the border.

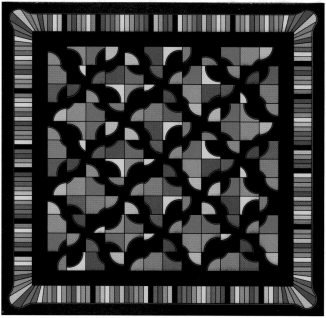

Dots Truly Gone, with *Leap Frog* border

As I planned the above corners for the quilt, my mind leaped back to other methods presented in this book. Suddenly, I've seen a way to make the borders even quicker, and to my way of thinking because it feels like a bit of a cheat, more fun. Why not make the borders into a big picture frame type of arrangement as outlined for the borders for *Gone Fishin'*, page 80?

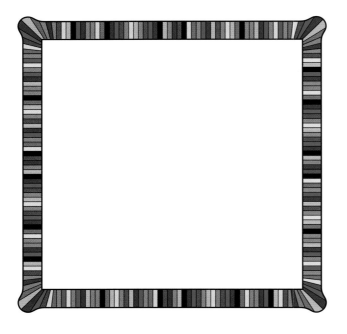

This reminds me of a quilt I designed very early when developing the bias bindings technique.

The straight segments used for the blocks in *Inchworm* made me think of using a straight border for *Dots Truly Gone* but there would be absolutely no reason that you couldn't use a wavy border in any of the ways explored through *Gone Fishin'*, page 80.

Showing *Inchworm* has made me want to show you three other quilts that Linda Park made to illustrate the use of this chapter's techniques. Linda, when you get tired of *Le Potager*, just pass it my way!

Dragonfly uses an oval-type shape instead of a circle and I do feel that using shapes other than circles is something I can look forward to exploring a great deal more or better still, to seeing what you do with them.

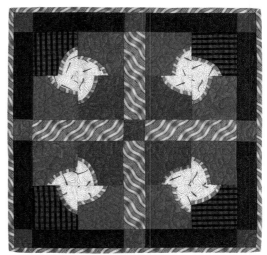

Dragonfly, 24'' x 24'', Linda Park, Westborough, Massachusetts

Inchworm, 92'' x 92'', Linda Park, Westborough, Massachusetts

Foolproof Curves

Le Potager, 60'' x 60'', Linda Park, Westborough, Massachusetts

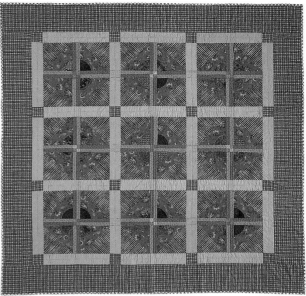

Blue, 85'' x 85'', Linda Park, Westborough, Massachusetts

As a final thought on this, I can't help wondering what would happen if I'd given *Dots Gone Crazy* a border treatment that is a sort of combination of *Le Potager* and *Kaleidoscope*, page 64.

This quilt would have to be called *Dots Gone Down a Kaleidoscope* or maybe *Dots Gone Over the Edge*.

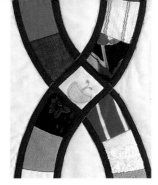

Jennifer's Quilt

Jennifer's Quilt, 82" x 74", Barbara Barber, Hampshire, England. Collection of Jack and Linda Parker, Kingsville, Texas

This is an exceedingly special quilt since it celebrates the life of Jennifer Parker 1972–2001. I want to tell you how this quilt came about and then I hope you see it for what it is—a happy quilt that reflects the life of a lovely, happy young woman. I also hope it touches your heart—it did mine.

Jack and Linda Parker are close family friends. They had a warm, loving family with two daughters, Jill and Jennifer, both in their twenties. Suddenly and most unexpectedly, Jennifer was taken from them while they were enjoying a family vacation away together. The devastation they felt was of a kind that is, thankfully for most of us, only the makings of nightmares.

I got an email from Jennifer's mother Linda. She said that they felt that the time had come for them to do something with Jennifer's clothes. She asked me if I knew of any quilt patterns that might be right for this sort of thing and also if I happened to know of a quilting shop near where she lives, half a world away from me, in south Texas, that might be able to make it for her family. I quickly dialed her telephone number and heard myself say, "Linda, I want to make this quilt for you." When the box of Jennifer's clothing arrived, I could acutely feel a mother's raw grief as I lifted the top item; a tiny baby dress.

I decided to use my bias binding techniques and a pieced chain that is part of the Double Wedding Ring pattern. Instead of using whole rings, I would use the sections where the rings overlapped to form the chains. I put my ideas to Jack and Linda: they were both deeply interested in every stage of the quilt's development.

Technically, there were bound to be many challenges when trying to combine such a wide range of fabrics. The whole gamut was there, everything from baby romper suits to evening dresses and woolen suits. There were pajamas, jeans, a terry cloth dressing gown, heavy sweaters, T-shirts, sweat shirts, silky dresses, cotton dresses, and a little rabbit suit to be worn for a little girl's first ballet recital.

How could I prevent distortion of the pieces during the making of the quilt? The only sensible approach was to stabilize it as I worked. For *Jennifer's Quilt*, I did not starch any of the fabrics; although if I were using normal quilting fabrics I would have given every fabric a really good stiff starching before cutting. Lightweight interfacing would be the answer. From the start I knew there would have to be a note on the label to dry clean only.

When cutting the pieces I was careful to be selective about what bits I used in order to make it more meaningful for her family. Tiny little appliqués from her baby clothes, the embroidered "Jennifer" from her high school sweater and logos on T-shirts from her first job as a speech therapist for children with learning difficulties, were some of the many treasures I could use to make this quilt unique.

Making *Jennifer's Quilt* was a uniquely special experience and please, as you read this do not feel sad. Working on it was anything but sad; poignant at times, yes, but I enjoyed the hours I spent reflecting Jennifer's life through these fabrics more than you can know. Linda and Jack now have the quilt in their family room as a quilt to be used and enjoyed in the true sense of the word "comforter."

Jennifer Parker

The chain goes on with Jennifer's little nephew, Parker Florence.

Materials

- **Navy Solid:** 6¼ yards for sashing strips, borders, bias binding, and edge binding
- **Cream Solid:** 1¾ yards for background of pieced strips
- **Assorted Fabrics:** 3 yards for the pieced chains and pieced border
- 5 yards for backing
- 87" x 79" batting
- **Lightweight Interfacing:** 3½ yards; this can be either iron-on or sew-in, polyester or cotton. If you use iron-on interfacing, be sure to make a sample because extra care must be taken with the foundation piecing in order to avoid getting all sorts of things gummed up, starting with the iron and then spreading it everywhere else.

NOTE: Interfacing is used instead of paper for the foundation patterns because unlike with most foundation piecing, you will not be removing the pattern; it serves as a vital stabilizer. On the other hand, if you wish to make this quilt with cotton fabrics, you could use paper photocopies for all of the chain units. In that case, you would remove the paper just before attaching to the cream fabric and handle these units with kid gloves to avoid distortion.

Photocopies

- 5 photocopies (or tracings) of the pattern for Jennifer's Chain, on pullout.

- Photocopy or trace pattern for Jennifer's Border, on pullout, overlapping the squares as you move along the design; 35 square segments each for the top and bottom edges of the quilt. For the sides, make 2 patterns with 41 segments.

Cutting

Navy Solid
- Cut 3 lengthwise strips 6½" x 58½" for sashing

- Cut 2 lengthwise strips 12½" x 58½" for side borders

- Cut 2 lengthwise strips 12½" x 74½" for top and bottom borders

- Cut 2 squares 32" x 32". Cut squares into 1¼"-wide bias strips for a total of approximately 1,586" of bias binding following the information in New Ideas and New Techniques, page 74.

Cream Solid
- Cut 4 lengthwise strips 8½" x 58½" for background of pieced strips.

Assorted Fabrics
- Cut 228 rectangles 3" x 3¾" for the pieced chain.

- Cut 152 squares 2½" x 2½" for the pieced border.

Preparing the Patterns

1. Overlap and glue photocopies of Jennifer's Chain pattern to form one long paper pattern for one whole section of the chain.

2. Use a fine-tip permanent pen to carefully draw a fine, dark line over the printed lines of the copies in order to allow you to see the pattern easily through the cream fabric and your chosen interfacing. You may not think this necessary but it really will help and, in most cases, will allow you to work without a light box although it would still probably be necessary with darker backgrounds.

3. Make foundation-piecing patterns. Trace half of the prepared chain pattern onto the interfacing, using the illustration as a guide.

Make 4.

4. Prepare the foundation patterns for the remaining sections of the chains. Tabs, such as those on paper-doll clothing, should be added to all of the flat, end pieces of the chains, both long and short. This tab should be roughly ³⁄₈" long and will serve as an extension under other sections. Continue to use the permanent pen throughout. Cut out the interfacing patterns exactly on the traced line.

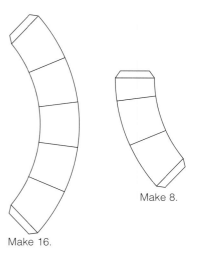

Make 16.

Make 8.

Foundation-Pieced Sections

1. Piece the chain units following the techniques in Curved-Unit Piecing, page 36. Tape the photocopy pattern for the chain to a flat surface.

2. Center a cream strip over the pattern and tape it down, as well. First, position the short units on the cream. I find that using a fabric glue stick for this makes it quick and easy but straight pins work equally well. The main thing is that the units must stay put until you can stitch them.

3. Sew the units in place, adding the binding to each edge. Do this with one line of stitching and refer to Sewing the Binding Onto Curved Shapes, page 77. Do this with all four of the cream strips.

Foolproof Curves

4. At this stage you can either finger-press the binding open or carefully use the tip of the iron to do so. Please learn from yet another of my mistakes and check your iron's settings if you are using mixed fabrics. I always leave my iron set full blast for my quilting and I managed to sizzle several pieces before it occurred to me that I had to turn down the temperature.

5. Re-position the cream strip over the paper pattern and attach the long chain units in the same way as the shorter ones. Now this may sound a little dubious but if the pieced unit does not fit absolutely perfectly, make it fit. Pull it into position and secure. If you are using normal quilting fabrics, this really should not be a problem but when you are using a mixed bunch it can tend to pull the chain in and make it seem just a touch too short in places. Pull it gently to stretch it back into shape and then secure to the cream background.

6. Attach the bias binding to this long section in the same way as for the shorter units. Take extra care to make certain that the binding on the shorter segments is turned outward when stitching the longer section in place. Complete all 4 chain units in this way.

Quilt Top Construction

1. Sew the cream chain strips together with the 6½" x 58½" navy strips in an alternating fashion. Press.

2. Refer to the quilt layout and then add the 12½" x 58½" navy strips, one to each side of the quilt top. Stitch the remaining 12½" x 74½" navy strips to the top and bottom, keeping the binding in position; I tend to either stitch or pin these in place.

Pieced Borders

1. Make foundation patterns for the pieced border. Do this in the same way as you did for the chain patterns. Be sure to add the tabs at the end of the patterns for the top and bottom edges.

2. Foundation piece the borders using the 2½" x 2½" pieces of assorted fabrics. The main reason for foundation piecing these is to stabilize the fabrics but another good reason is for consistency. In many cases, consistency is the key to good workmanship. The chains were made using a certain process and in order to give the quilt the best long-term quality finish the same sort of process should be applied to its borders. With this in mind, the pieced borders will not be sewn onto navy borders with a seam but will be appliquéd on in the same way as the chains. The only real difference is that you should use the bias binding technique on the inner edge of the border but not on the outer edge because that will be bound in the standard way, using binding, as you would any of your quilts.

3. At the corners, the bindings cross over each other to give a balanced effect.

Corner Border

This was easily achieved using the partial seaming method when attaching the bias binding along the top and bottom edges. Start and stop the stitching about 1" in from the edges when attaching the bias binding to the first two edges and also be sure to leave a 3" tail of excess binding at both ends. Add the remaining foundation units onto the sides in the normal way, taking care to keep the shorter loose ends of binding out of the seamline.

4. Finger-press this final binding outward, pin in position if desired, and then lay the loose ends of binding down over the top and stitch in place, giving a crisscross effect.

Finishing

1. Trace Jennifer's Quilting Pattern onto the quilt top before layering and quilting.

2. Layer and baste the quilt.

3. Bind with 2"-wide bias strips cut from a 27" x 27" square.

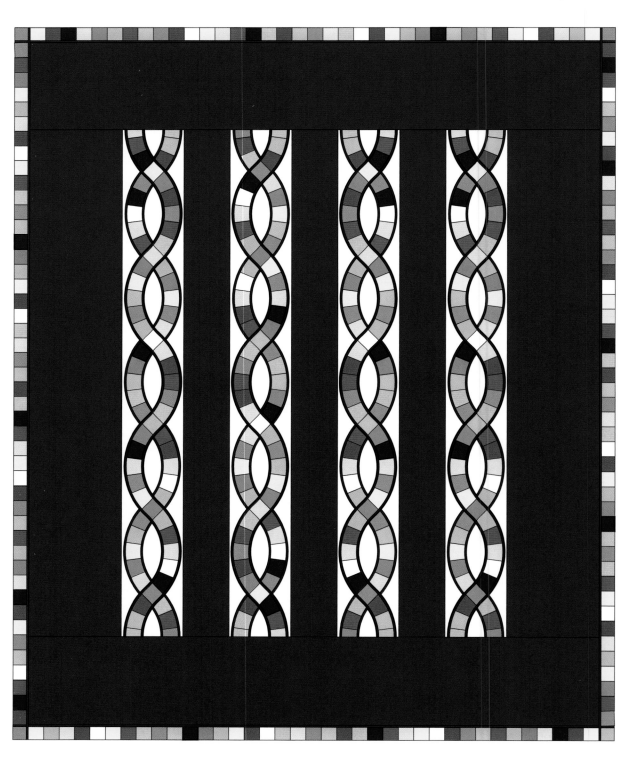

What Ifs

Consider what you could do with this type of "stripey" quilt layout combined with binding and Really Sharp Piecing techniques. With widespread appeal, stripey quilts are as old as the hills and you should tackle them with the same "what if" sort of approach as any other form of design. Let one rough drawing lead to another and I think you will be quite amazed at how much fun it is and be surprised where you end up.

I use this process for most of my quilts. As an exercise using *Jennifer's Quilt*, that's exactly what I did and as always, when I play this game, I am totally dumbfounded as to how one gets from A to B, so to speak. In the drawings below, I would like to share my thoughts and design processes exactly as they occurred to me. I don't pretend they're great, just a process of one thing leading to another and what is more, I personally think that the final quilt, combined with lots of appliquéd flowers from my book *Flower Power*, is possibly another one to add to my ever lengthening list of quilts I need to make.

My rough drawings are *very* rough indeed and my dear husband Peter would be the first to vouch for that if he wasn't far too much of a gentleman to say so. Because of that, I'd like to take this opportunity to give him a *very* big hug and kiss to say thank you. After all, not only has he been the best husband for the past 25 years but also the best, and most patient draftsman, since I started quilting half a marriage ago!

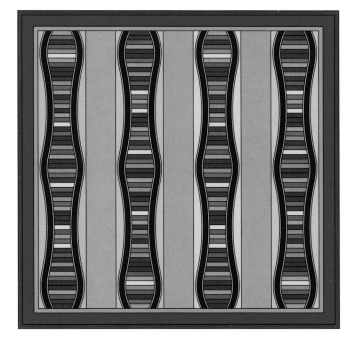

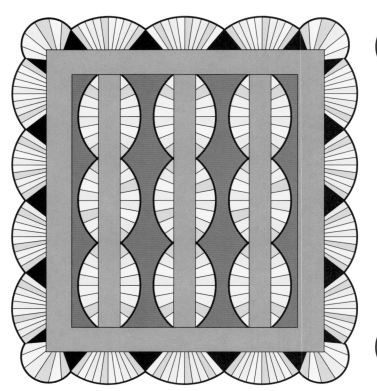

Foolproof Curves

The Baker's Dozen

Writing this book has been a much greater pleasure for me than I anticipated and I think the reason is that I feel like I have been sharing with friends. I've truly enjoyed your company and ask you to indulge me just a little bit longer as I delve into another one of my passions. People who know me well are aware that I have a passion for baking; all sorts of baking, but especially cakes. So much so, that John Payne, the head of our local council, threatens, after each of his visits to my house, to have a sign erected outside saying "EXQUISITE CAKES WITHIN." John makes these visits on a variety of pretenses, but Peter and I have long suspected them to be cake-sampling missions. It's a jolly good thing we're very fond of him!

Cooking, like sewing, has always been part of my life and for years, I did more cooking than sewing. In 1991, a life-changing event took place: I started quilting. Cooking was shoved to the back burner, resulting in many burnt offerings. I buried myself in quilting, enjoying every minute of it. Thankfully, the supermarkets rescued me with prepared meals. Alas, I burned even these and dear Peter, who can't boil an egg, took over out of self-preservation: after all, someone had to survive this Quilting Bug if for no other reason than to pay the fabric bills!

Experience shows my problems aren't unique but just part of the Quilting Bug. There is no cure but I want to convince even the skeptical to bake a cake—just one for a start. You can do both and that's what this recipe is all about. The rewards are great! People suddenly see you in a new light because you can quilt *and* cook. Another word of warning, this delicious cake is so easy to make you won't even notice that you are cooking and therein lies the danger; before you know it, you're making another and who knows where that might lead. One thing is certain, it *won't* stop you quilting and the "what ifs" of both are the most fun and creative.

This cake has gone through rigorous testing on both sides of the Atlantic and my trusty Cake Samplers, husband Peter and Councilor John Payne, have several observations. They say Lime Juice Icing is an absolute *must* and that to get the best flavor it must be kept 24–48 hours to "chill out." It was quite amusing watching these sophisticated older gentlemen discussing the necessity for a cake to chill out!

Orange and Raisin Cake

- 260 grams or 2 cups raisins
- 200 grams or 1 cup orange juice
- Grated rind of one large orange
- 4 large eggs
- 350 grams or 1³⁄₄ cups sugar
- 300 grams or 1¹⁄₃ cups of softened butter
- 450 grams or 3¹⁄₂ cups self–rising flour
- 1–4 tablespoons milk

*Use either grams or cups throughout–don't switch between.

Put raisins and juice into a large bowl and leave for 1–2 days. Add remaining ingredients to the raisins, beating well. Add milk in stages to give a soft, dropping consistency. A spoonful of mixture should drop from the spoon when tapped on the bowl.

Spoon the mixture into a greased and floured bunt tin or two loaf tins. Pop into 350° F oven and bake 1–1¹⁄₄ hours; it should feel firm and a tester will come out clean. Let cool half an hour before turning onto rack. Ice when cold.

For lime icing, dilute powdered sugar with lime juice to give the consistency you prefer and drizzle over the cake.

A Cure-All

For me, baking has become a panacea for most things ranging from worry about one's offspring, to quilt designs, to writer's block, to a wonderfully soothing cure for jetlag. I'm sure, given a chance, you too will find baking to be a splendid remedy for at least one of life's little problems. The trait of seeking consolation in the oven does also seem an inherited characteristic. During times of duress, my dearest Auntie Clara always reaches for her mixing bowls with fantastic results. But then again, her Danish mother, my paternal grandmother, had a cake for every occasion. We thought she was just a good cook; now I know she got as much out of it as we did.

I do hope you enjoy making this cake but if you're unconvinced, just keep making the quilts! Finally, I've one more theory, for each quilt you make, I like to think it will take one off my list of quilts I need to make, thereby giving me time to bake another cake while dreaming up yet one more quilt to add to my list!

About the Author

Barbara Barber lives in southern rural Britain and shares her life with husband Peter and daughter Eliza along with their beloved dogs Mildred and Gertrude. Jacob, their Maine Coon cat keeps them all in order. Self–taught, Barbara started quilting in May 1991 by making a quilt to match her bedroom curtains. The fascination has never diminished and now, having won many major international awards and teaching, lecturing, and judging, she has traveled all over the world. The thing that maintains her interests is a constant search to develop new techniques that allow quilters of all levels to more easily make complex looking quilts with a quality finish.

Index

Other Fine books from C&T Publishing

For more information, ask for a free catalog:
C&T Publishing, Inc.
P.O. Box 1456
Lafayette, CA 94549
(800) 284-1114
Email: ctinfo@ctpub.com
Website: www.ctpub.com

For quilting supplies:
Cotton Patch Mail Order
3405 Hall Lane, Dept. CTB
Lafayette, CA 94549
(800) 835-4418
(925) 283-7883
Email: quiltusa@yahoo.com
Website: www.quiltusa.com

Note: Fabrics used in the quilts shown may not be currently available because fabric manufacturers keep most fabrics in print for only a short time.